Blind Courage

Christine Deponio   *Part 1*

Love from
Christine x

First published in Great Britain as a softback original in 2013

Copyright © Christine Deponio 2013

The moral right of this author has been asserted.

Typeset in Allure and ITC New Baskerville

Proofreading, design and publishing by Consilience Media

www.consil.co.uk

ISBN: 978-0-9926433-4-8

Dedication

I am dedicating this book to my wonderful husband Raymond and to my two precious sons Lee and Ryan. Thank you for being my towers of strength and for all your love and support over the years. You have both grown into fine young independent men of whom I'm so proud. You are my life and my shining lights in a dark world.

I love you more than words can ever say and will always be there for you.

Note to the reader

I apologise for the small amount of strong language in this book as I don't wish to offend anyone.

I felt that it was necessary for it to be put in as I have to be truthful not just to myself but also to you readers about my thoughts and actions as I have to say it as it was.

All the words in this book are entirely my own. Nothing has been edited or changed by anyone and no ghost writer has been involved at all.

Please note, every effort has been made to contact copyright holders of any photographs used prior to publication.

Foreword

I hope by reading this book it will bring you strength and comfort
in knowing you are not alone as I have been there, done that and
have came out of the other side and so can you. I have learnt over
the years that we can't live our lives in the past otherwise we will
destroy ourselves forever.

It's about here and now and not dwelling on the things that
we can't do and once used to, it's about thinking and focusing on
what we can do and are still very capable of if we put our minds to
it. Never give up on yourself and always remember that we are all
equal in this world, no one being better than the other. There were
times in my life when I just wanted to die, give up and throw the
towel in but that would have been the easy way out.

The world can be our oyster and life is what we make of it as it is
up to us which pathway we choose to go down. I feel that everything
in life is about love, caring for one another, sharing everything
that we have and giving hope and encouragement to others for the
future.

I have had to fight with all my might throughout life as nothing
comes on a silver platter. Always believe in yourself and remember
that everything is possible. Stand tall, be strong, go forward and
don't look back.

I pray and hope that all of your dreams and wishes come true.

Yours
Christine

Contents

Chapter 1

In the summer of 1970, at the age of sixteen, I was rushed into the Queen Elizabeth Hospital, Gateshead. Everything happened so quickly and little did I know then, that in a matter of weeks I would be left without sight. In 1969, at the age of fifteen, I had left school and gone to work at Boots the Chemist, as a shop assistant, in my local town, Gateshead. Everyone was friendly and it had a nice atmosphere when I walked in. I really enjoyed working there; it was a great shop – much different from today, as there were many different departments, and I worked with a fab bunch of girls.

I left for work as usual that morning to catch the 8:30 bus, as I started at 9:00. I didn't feel any different that day to any other day; at least that's what I thought. Little did I know (or even anyone else for that matter), that this would be my last day ever to work in Boots the Chemist.

I arrived that morning and went upstairs to the locker room and changed into my uniform as usual and then went down to my department which was fancy goods, selling jewellery, handbags, glassware etc. Everything was normal and I felt fine. We had a tea break in the morning. I always enjoyed and looked forward to having a good old chinwag with the girls as well as a cup of tea and a chocolate biscuit.

Dinner time was always the highlight of the day when we all got together and just laughed and giggled, telling stories and jokes and catching up with all the gossip from the night before. It was all just good clean innocent fun. When most of them had finished their lunch, out came the make-up. I used to be fascinated at how quickly they could make their eyes up. I was just a plain Jane and had never worn make up before – and still don't today.

Two of the girls, Linda and Kath, who had short hair, bought long wigs. They were fantastic and looked so real, I couldn't believe the transformation when they put them on. They were all good looking girls and very fashionable, while I was still wearing some of my older sister's cast-offs. However, this didn't bother me as I came from a big family and money was tight in those days.

When lunch was over, a horrible ill feeling came over me – although I could still hear the girls laughing in the background. It is difficult to put into words exactly how I felt and I could not understand what was happening to me. I remember feeling as if my head was going to burst open at any minute and I couldn't think straight. I began to feel numb; I was very frightened, confused and felt totally out of control. After that, nothing appeared to be clear in my mind and I remember hearing people shouting. I felt as if my body was being dragged about. I must have fallen into a state of unconsciousness, and much later I found myself waking up in the Queen Elizabeth Hospital, in a straightjacket with a tube stuck down my throat and my stomach was being pumped.

I began to be sick, and voices kept shouting at me asking what tablets I had taken and how many. At this time nothing was making sense. I couldn't understand what was going on at all, and I remember nothing more until I woke up in Dunston Hill Hospital, which is just up the road from where I lived.

It was a large wooden hut, which was one of the old army barrack wards and it was a very dreary and drab looking dormitory with approximately 27 old wrought iron army beds filled with sick, elderly people.

I found it hard to settle in as it was the first time I had ever been in hospital. I had only been in a few days when three people died. One patient was next to me and two were on the opposite side of the ward. I was terrified. It really upset me, more so because I was only sixteen, just a child really. What a terrible place for anyone to be put in at such a young age.

CHAPTER 1

The doctor who came to see me on the ward was horrible; he was cold, rude and very abrupt and never smiled once. There were times when he had me in tears because of his manner and he never apologised – even the nurses looked frightened of him and said very little. I watched him very carefully to see how he dealt with the other patients. I thought because they were elderly and very poorly he might have had more compassion and respect for them, but I was wrong. He really was a 'nasty piece of work' and not even fit to be called a doctor as far as I was concerned.

After eight or nine days I took another one of those horrible bad turns. This is the only way I can describe and recall them. I just can't fully remember what happened. I began to open my eyes but could only manage to keep them open for a very short period of time and felt so tired. I hadn't a clue where I was and felt totally disorientated. While lying there everything was so bright and fuzzy, the room felt as if it was moving all over the place – I thought that at any minute it was going to collapse. I remember feeling as though I was going to be sick, and tried to turn over but couldn't as my body felt like a ton weight, as if somebody was sitting on me. Suddenly these faces seemed to appear from nowhere and were moving in slow motion. I could hear voices – it was all very weird. Someone then turned me over and put my head into a bowl as I had started to be sick. Afterwards I kept trying to sit up, but everything was such an effort.

I have never drank alcohol or taken drugs – for example cannabis, happy baccy etc – apart from medication prescribed by my GP. Yet the way I was feeling was as if I was as high as a kite and stoned out of my mind without a care in the world. I still lay there for a little while and my eyes now were beginning to focus better and my mind was becoming much clearer. I could see there were two nurses sitting at my bedside, but they never said a word. I began to look round the room and thought how odd it looked as I had never seen one like this before, let alone been in one. I wondered where the window and doors were as I couldn't find one anywhere – still I was wondering where I was.

The nurses continued to sit and still hadn't spoken – in saying that, neither had I. I thought to myself, am I dreaming or is this really happening? All of a sudden I caught a glimpse of something in the corner of the room which drew my attention. When I looked again I realised it was the shape of a door which I thought looked very odd. My eyes then focused on the tiny pane of glass at the top of the door which I stared at fiercely. I then shot out of the bed like somebody not right when I realised there were bars on it. I startled the nurses so much that they leapt to their feet, quicker than ever. What a fright they must have had. I went off balance and fell flat on my face onto the floor, after which the nurses bent down and picked me up. I was in a total state of shock and literally shaking from head to foot with fear, shouting "Where the hell am I?" "What on earth am I doing here?" "Tell me where I am." It was only then I realised I had been lying on a mattress on the floor and not in a proper bed. I was so frightened I began to cry and wished that my mam was there – or at least somebody with me.

Shortly afterwards the nurses then took me from the room, and as they escorted me down the corridor my body felt weak and wobbly. They took me into what looked like an office and introduced me to a female doctor. She was very gentle when she spoke to me. She told me I was in a hospital called St Mary's at Stannington, which meant nothing to me as I had never heard of it before. She explained that the room I had slept in was known as a 'padded cell', where they had put me because I was ill.

Again even that went over my head because I had never heard of a padded cell before, and certainly didn't know at the time what they were used for.

"You do know that you were transferred here from Dunston Hill three and a half days ago?" explained the doctor.

"What do you mean, I've been here for three and a half days?" I replied. How can anyone be in a place three and a half days and not remember anything about it? I was beginning to feel very anxious and agitated about it all.

She explained to me: "At Dunston Hill, Christine, you took ill and they had to sedate you with a tranquilizer, which is an injection that helps to put you to sleep, and we have also had to keep you sedated here for a while."

After hearing that I just sat there; I didn't know what to say, what to do, what questions to ask, or what else to even talk about. I just felt totally lost and alone. After the interview I was then taken to the shower block which certainly could have done with a make-over. There were toilets on one side and open showers on the other. I was told to go to the toilet then to undress and have a quick shower. After I had been to the toilet, the nurse then said, "Come along Christine, we haven't got all day you know."

"Are you not going to leave the room?" I asked quietly.

"I can't do that because of safety precautions," she replied.

"What do you mean 'safety precautions'?"

"It's just in case anything happens to you and to make sure that you're alright."

"What could possibly happen to me?" I replied. "I'm only going to have a shower."

I had never felt so embarrassed standing there naked in front of a complete stranger while she watched me undress and shower myself down. How humiliating it was.

After my shower I was taken into a large dayroom. The nurse told me to go and find a seat and that dinner wouldn't be long and that I would hear a bell ring. I couldn't believe that she had just walked away and left me there like that. It was a very large, pleasant room. It was hot and the sun was shining; there were huge bay windows which overlooked the most beautiful gardens. There were many other people of all ages sitting in armchairs that were scattered in different parts of the room. I didn't quite know what to make of it all. Everyone looked as if they were fast asleep. There seemed to be no life anywhere at all, which seemed rather strange and I felt a little bit nervous.

All of a sudden a girl came to the door. She looked older than I was and also looked ill. Her face was pale, she was very thin and her clothes looked as if they were two sizes too big for her. She had uncombed ginger hair and her fringe just hung over her eyes – it looked as if she could have done with a good haircut. It was a shame really as she had a bonnie face. She saw that I was looking at her and she smiled, came over and sat beside me.

"Hi, my name's Angela – what's yours? I'm twenty-one – how old are you?"

At first I didn't notice there was anything wrong with her; she made me feel so much at ease. It was good to talk to someone who wasn't much older than I was. A few minutes later, a nurse came in with a very large bell and began to ring it.

"Dinnertime everybody, dinner time," she shouted. Generally speaking it was like being back at school. I was amazed to see how many people jumped up. One minute they were zonked out and the next, they were standing to attention. You had to see it to believe it.

We walked down the corridor to the dining room and I noticed how nobody seemed to speak to each other; some were shuffling, others looked as if they were drunk, walking from one side of the corridor to the other. Some were making funny noises while others were grunting, and Angela was holding on to my arm for grim death. My mind was now beginning to bobble. As we entered the dining room everyone just seemed to know where to sit and Angela was making sure I was sitting beside her.

Dinner wasn't served immediately, and boy I wished it had. Angela was now playing with my hair with one hand, and stroking my arm with the other. Some were beginning to bang their hands on the table, others were stamping their feet. It was then that I realised there was obviously something wrong with these people.

CHAPTER 1

The noises began to get louder and louder, I started to feel panicky and my mind was racing fifty to the dozen. *My goodness me, I'm in a flaming loony bin* I thought to myself, *a bloody loony bin. What the hell am I doing in a place like this, what the hell am I doing in here? I shouldn't be in a place like this. Somebody's made a big mistake by putting me in here* – that's all that kept going over and over in my mind. I could literally feel myself breaking out in a cold sweat. My heart was beating faster. I was speechless. I was frightened to move or even lift my head to look about and see what was going on, so I just kept my eyes fixed down on the table.

Then three or four nurses came running in to try and get things under control. And boy did some of them get a telling off. Dinner was now being served and after all that I wasn't feeling very hungry. Just when I thought things were starting to calm down, I couldn't believe what happened next. There was this massive eruption. Some of the patients began to tip tables over while others smashed chairs through the bay windows. It was so terrifying. I thought things only happened like this on TV, but never in real life. There was glass all over and dinner everywhere in a matter of seconds. I couldn't believe the state the room was in. The noise was horrendous, patients were shouting and shrieking.

Nurses came and took me out of the room. Apparently the same female doctor that I had seen earlier that morning wanted to see me again in her office. This time she asked me lots of different questions. I can't remember what they were but there were also puzzles to do. At the end of what seemed to be a very long interview, she sat back and looked at me, then she said, "You know, Christine, I cannot understand why you have been put in here. I don't even know who transferred you from Dunston Hill Hospital to this one. I don't know who was responsible, but all I know is I feel you should not be in here and especially not in this section. Do you realise what type of hospital you're in and exactly where you are?"

I said, "I have a vague idea after what's just happened in the dining room."

"This part of the hospital is for people who are sick and mentally ill and some of the people have been sectioned here for many years and will most probably never go home again, as they are here for their own protection as well as that of others. Now what I am going to do, Christine, is transfer you over to another part of the hospital where people aren't so poorly."

Within a matter of hours I was transferred over. When I arrived at the other part of the hospital there was quite a wide range of age groups. Some were listening to music while others were in groups, talking or watching TV. I somehow felt so relieved to be away from that other part of the hospital, but I would have much rather been at home. It didn't take long to settle in – everyone was so friendly and made a point of making me feel so welcome.

Many of the patients were married and had children, some even had grandchildren. There were those who were suffering from manic depression, breakdowns and some with other disorders. A lot of them were still finding it hard to cope and deal with the many traumatic things that had happened to them. For example: mental abuse, sexual abuse which leaves scars, heartache and pain. The mind is a funny thing. It can sometimes only take so much before it snaps. How do I know? Because I was one of those people.

I wished I could have been in the dormitory with the other patients instead of having to share a small bedroom with two elderly ladies who looked as if they were going to die at any minute. Their hair was almost white and their skin was very wrinkled and they were lying there with their eyes and mouths wide open and no teeth in. It wasn't pleasant at all – it was quite frightening. It's not that I didn't like elderly people, because I do, but with being so young and having to sleep in the next bed to them when they were so ill was a very different matter.

My bed was next to a large window that looked into the nurse's office. It felt like they were watching every move I made, and it made me feel very uncomfortable. I would sometimes just sit on my bed and look out onto the gardens. The windows stretched across the whole room from floor to ceiling. The gardens were spectacular with well kept lawns and lots of beautiful flower beds.

Sometimes the days could be very long especially when I didn't have any visitors. I only had a visit once a week. There wasn't very much to do there – you could read or write, watch TV or listen to the radio. After a while it could become quite boring. Although everyone was friendly I was the youngest one there – everyone seemed to be a lot older than I was. At times I was lonely and I felt a little out of place. I used to look forward to my Auntie Florrie coming in to see me. She was my mam's sister and they would both visit every Saturday. Auntie Florrie used to always lift my spirits and make me feel good as she used to make me laugh. I would get a big hug and some goodies off her which made me feel special. I hated it when she had to leave. I was sometimes lucky if my mam said hello or even goodbye.

It was about nine pm and we hadn't long finished supper, the medication had been given out and the last thing I remember it was almost time for bed. I just woke up feeling a little confused and again not quite sure where I was. I tried to move but I couldn't. It was then I realised I was injured. I was lying face down on a hard cold floor wearing only a short nightdress. I could feel my head and face swelling up and the trickling of blood running down into my mouth.

The room was dim, but I could see there was a light shining above me from the right hand side. I managed to move my head only slightly; the pain was unbearable and I thought I was going to pass out. Then I saw it, there it was, the great big steel door with a little window with bars on it. Yeah, now I knew exactly where I was. I vaguely remember being dragged from my bed again and being thrown into this horrible godforsaken padded cell. I hated it in there and I didn't know why they kept doing this. I began to shout for help and hoped someone would hear me as the cell was down the other end of the corridor on its own, away from the other wards and everyone else. I tried so hard to move my arms and body so I could try to push myself up off the floor, but I just couldn't do it.

Eventually a nurse came and I managed to move my head slightly and look up at the door and saw her face at the window.

"Get into bed, Christine," she shouted! "Get into bed now." By the way, the bed was a mattress on the floor with a pillow and a couple of blankets chucked on it.

I shouted, "I can't move, I can't get up, I'm injured, I'm bleeding and I need someone to help me." She wouldn't listen or take any notice of what I was saying to her and still kept shouting from outside the door.

"Get into bed, Christine and I mean now."

She couldn't help but see I was injured from where I was lying. I couldn't believe it when I heard her footsteps walking away from the door and back down the corridor. There was no one else but me. I was so frightened I began to cry.

I was now beginning to feel ill and felt too weak to shout any more, and thought I was going to die. Quietly I began to say to myself *I don't want to die, I don't want to die here on my own.* I remember I began to pray to God although I didn't even believe in him; as a matter of fact I was very angry and bitter, and blamed God for everything that had happened to me in my life. Yet here I was saying over and over again, *please God, don't let me die here on my own.* Looking back I feel it was so inhumane to have left me there like that. After all I was only sixteen years old, just a child really, especially in those days. It just should never have happened.

The next thing I remember was being awakened by the jingling and rattling of keys knocking against the cell door as they unlocked it. It was now morning and I was still lying in the same position as the night before. I don't know if I had passed out or maybe just drifted off to sleep. My head and face felt huge and they were throbbing. I licked my lips which were sore and swollen. I was cold and soaking wet as I was lying in my own urine.

Apparently I had been lying there approximately ten hours. I was just so pleased to be alive. Not that they were bothered though – they couldn't have given a toss whether I lived or died. I was still feeling ill and weak and really didn't have the energy to speak. Two nurses came into the cell. They never uttered a word or even asked how I was. They physically grabbed an arm each and bodily dragged me out of that cell and down the corridor. And when I say dragged I literally mean physically being dragged with my body and legs trailing across the floor. The faster they walked while dragging me, the pain in my head became more intense. It felt as if it was bouncing all over the place. My arms were hurting, my whole body was hurting. I no longer felt like a human being, but like an animal that's being taken away to be slaughtered. Suddenly the nurses stopped, then everything happened so quickly.

A blanket was wrapped around me, then I heard a man's voice saying, "I've got her now."

He picked me up and carried me into the ambulance. The sirens were going and then I opened my eyes. There were a couple of ambulance men sitting there. I remember nothing more until I woke up in the Newcastle General Hospital where I was being pushed down the corridor on a trolley. Eventually they stopped the trolley and pushed it against a wall. It was so quiet and there was nobody else about bar the porters. I was feeling frightened, anxious and agitated because I didn't know what was going to happen to me as nobody had explained or said anything yet. Then this young woman came over to me and the porters then left. She had shoulder-length hair; it was dark and it was difficult to tell how old she was. She was small in stature but rather plump and was wearing a long white coat. She didn't even have the damn courtesy to explain what she was going to do or even what was going to happen next. She really was just abrupt, rude and heartless. She literally yanked my arm so hard and pulled me up into a sitting position, whipped my nightie off and shoved a white gown on me. I thought I was going to throw up all over her, and what a pity I hadn't. Throwing up all over her would have suited me fine as she bloody well deserved it. She pushed the trolley into what seemed like a huge room and when I looked around all I could see was lots of equipment, instruments and apparatus. It was then I realised I was in an operating theatre.

I totally flipped my lid. I shrieked and shouted at the top of my voice. "What are you doing, what on earth are you going to do?"

I just kept repeating myself over and over again. I was absolutely terrified, which certainly didn't help the way I was feeling. Then that same horrible bitch of a woman – because that's exactly what she was, a bloody bitch – started smacking my face from side to side and began to shout at me.

"You stupid girl, will you stop shouting like that and being so ridiculous? For goodness sake, you're sixteen years of age, not six."

I just couldn't help myself, I was in a total state of shock. She couldn't help but notice the state my head and face were in and must've known how I was feeling.

It takes a lot to rile me and make me angry, but I was so absolutely furious with her that I literally wanted to jump off that couch and smash her face in and see how the hell she liked it. She was a bastard.

Then all of a sudden an older man appeared who was wearing a long white coat. He was tall and slim with silver grey hair and a beard. At first I thought he had only come to see what all the noise and commotion was about, because you couldn't have helped but hear it. It turned out he was the anaesthetist and boy did he put this nurse in her place. I could tell he was absolutely furious with her for the way that I had been treated. She probably thought because she was on her own and I was only sixteen that she could just treat me any old how and get away with it. But boy, that was the biggest

CHAPTER 1

mistake she ever made as nobody should ever be allowed to treat someone like that. I knew by the tone of the anaesthetist's voice that she was going to be in deep trouble. I was so pleased about that. The anaesthetist was a lovely man and he could see how disturbed and upset I was.

He apologised and remarked, "You should never have been brought into the operating theatre, Christine, the way you had been."

He then pushed the trolley back out of the operating theatre and back into the corridor where he tried to calm me down. He then gently took my hand, smiled at me and began to stroke my arm. His voice was so gentle and reassuring and he kept asking me to relax and not to worry about anything as I was now in safe hands and that everything was going to be fine.

He explained how I needed an operation to see if I had a brain tumour.

"We need to do some deep head X-rays, Christine, and to do that we need to put you to sleep. It will only take an hour and you will be back on the ward before you know it."

I had never had an operation before and I was frightened at the thought of being put to sleep. It's amazing how many thoughts flash through you mind in a matter of seconds. *What if I don't wake up? What will I be like after the operation?* It was so scary just knowing that for a short period of time that someone else was going to be in control of my life rather than me. Yet when I looked at the anaesthetist's face his warm smile made me feel safe and reassured me that I trusted him entirely.

I could feel myself being sick and felt somebody sticking a bowl underneath my chin and wiping my mouth. Then I heard a voice in the distance saying, "Christine, wake up, Christine, it's time to wake up now. It's almost four thirty in the morning."

I remember trying so hard to open up my eyes but I just couldn't as they felt like lumps of lead. I was still being sick, and the voice kept repeating over and over again, "Christine, wake up, it's almost four thirty in the morning and we need you to wake up now."

The next thing I felt was someone tapping the side of my cheek. It might have been a tap to them but I thought somebody was hitting me with a sledge hammer and I thought my head was going to fall off my shoulders at any minute. I remember grabbing the nurse's arm, I held it tight and was squeezing it as hard as I could. She woke me up alright and the pain was unbearable. I gritted my teeth together and forced myself to speak.

"Stop hitting my face. I mean it. Stop hitting my face now."

I was now slowly beginning to open my eyes. Next, the nurse switched the lamp on above my head. I screamed as it felt as if someone was putting red hot pokers into my eyes and literally pulling them out.

"Turn those fucking lights out," I shouted at the top of my voice. "They're burning me eyes out man, turn them out."

I don't know what happened after that – they may have given me a sedative to help me relax and deal with the pain or maybe I had just drifted off to sleep.

I could hear the clattering of dishes and people talking and laughing and the sound of trolleys being wheeled up and down the corridor. I was now beginning to wake up and thought it must be morning time as I could smell the cooking of breakfast. I was in a small side room on my own lying flat on my back with cot sides up at both sides of the bed. The curtains were still closed which helped to dim the light and my head and eyes were feeling much better than they had been earlier that morning. Then the nurse came in to see if I was awake and how I was feeling. I asked if she was the same nurse who had attended to me earlier when I first woke up and she replied yes. I apologized for my bad behaviour and foul language and asked if her arm was alright.

"I know you were only doing your job and you probably weren't tapping my face too hard and it was certainly out of character the way I behaved. I can't begin to express the amount of pain I was in. I truly felt as if my head was just being torn off and my eyes were being ripped out."

She explained that she was the one who should be apologizing and not me. "Because at the time, Christine, I wasn't aware of everything that had happened or what had been done to you, and didn't realize the amount of pain you would be in."

The nurse then left the room and suddenly there was a knock at the door and an elderly lady came to say hello. She leaned on the cot sides and asked: "What's your name, love and what are you in for?"

"My name is Christine," I replied. "I've just had some deep head X-rays done yesterday."

"Are you sure about that, love?"

"Well yes, that's what they said it was," I said.

"Well I've been up since first thing this morning and have given some other patients a cup of tea and I had the same operation as you had yesterday. So I can't understand how I'm up walking about and you're lying there like that flat on your back. It just doesn't make sense, pet. I'll tell you what to do, love. When the nurse or doctor comes in to see you later ask them again what type of operation you've had done and I'll come back later to find out, because if you've had the same operation as me there's something gone far wrong here, luvvy".

Not long after she left, in walked a young black dishy male nurse – when he spoke and smiled his whole face seemed to light up.

"Good morning Christine and how are we this morning?"

"Much better than I was earlier."

"Good," he replied then he went down to the bottom of the bed.

At first I wasn't too sure what he was doing. He then pulled the blankets back from the bottom of the bed and I saw him pull something out with his hand. When I saw it was my dirty sanitary towel my face went beetroot. I was speechless and I felt so embarrassed that I wished the floor would have opened up there and then and swallowed me up. He then took a clean one out of another bag and put it between my legs and said, "Right Christine, I'll come back later to turn you over."

Turn me over? I thought, *what on earth is he talking about, turn me over?* I was so confused. Why couldn't I feel what he was doing to me!

I was absolutely horrified and so upset about what had just happened.

He may have been a male nurse and was only doing his job but it still didn't make me feel any better.

I found out later that he was only nineteen years old, three years older than me. I am certainly not a prude, but I hope the medical profession today have got their act together because they certainly hadn't all those years ago. Something as personal as that should never have happened.

As I had only been awake for a short period of time and was only able to move my arms and head, it wasn't until the nurses came back to turn me over as they put it, that suddenly I realised that I was paralysed from the chest down. Nobody had the sense, brains, or intelligence to have come and explained that. I couldn't believe that all of this was happening to me – my life just seemed to be going from bad to worse. I was beginning to think and hope that this was all just a horrible nightmare, a real bad dream and that at any minute I would wake up and that everything would be just fine, but it wasn't a bad dream, it was real alright. How I wish my Nana Gardner was still alive and here beside me now so she could just give me a big hug and hold me tight and to tell me not to worry, and that everything would be alright, but I knew that wasn't going to happen. *Even my mam's not here but that's nothing out of the ordinary.* She was never there for me and she certainly wouldn't know how to comfort me. How I wish I could go back to where I was born.

Chapter 2

I was born at 37 Back–Villa Place in Newcastle upon Tyne. The seven years we lived there were the most happiest and cherished memories of my life. I was born on the 30th of December 1953 to my parents Jean and John Pattinson. I had an older sister called Jacqueline who was two and a half years older and my twin brother John.

We lived together in a small upstairs two bedroomed flat with a scullery and a kitchen, which today is known as the sitting room or a lounge if you're posh. Auntie Florrie, my mother's sister, and my Uncle Gordon lived downstairs. We shared a backyard and an outdoor toilet. I loved my Auntie Florrie; she was great. She played with all the children in the street and joined in many of the games. She taught me how to play 'two baller', 'skippies', 'elastics' and many other games. I used to love playing 'hopscotch', 'piggy in the middle' and 'chucks'. They were certainly the days. We knew how to play, not like the children today.

Where I lived the streets were long and cobbled and had back lanes. It was brilliant; I loved it – they had so much character. We would run up and down the streets with our hula hoops and playing with our marbles. I never went anywhere without them. I was about five or six when yo-yos came out and my Uncle Gordon was a dab hand at the yo-yo and taught us many tricks.

We had old fashioned gas lamps in the streets where we lived. I used to love watching the gas man when he came round with his big long ladders. He stood them against the lamp, climbed up and opened the glass window to light the lamps. They would look so pretty and beautiful. Neighbours were neighbours in those days. Everyone was so friendly and nobody had more than anybody else.

At least, where I lived they didn't. It was a much slower pace of life in those days. Mums and grandparents would be sitting on street walls or standing at the door chatting to each other. The women wore pinnies and turbans. My mam used to wear a green one and the older men would be dressed in suits and wearing caps and many of them would have a cigarette hanging from their mouths while talking. On certain days most of the women would be down on their hands and knees scrubbing their steps with this yellow stone and buffing it up. Many of them took it seriously and tried to present the best step.

In those days many people didn't have much money and I remember going to the corner shop to buy a pound in weight of chocomix and that would be our ration of sweets for the week between the three of us. My mam would give each of us a little white paper bag and put eight or nine Choco mix sweets in each day. The highlight of the week for me was when we went to visit our grandparents on a Sunday, my Nana and Granda Gardner, my mam's mam and dad. They didn't live very far away from us – it was a ten to fifteen minute walk from where we lived. They also lived in a two bedroomed upstairs flat. Although they didn't have very much either, it was a much nicer flat than ours as it was brighter, slightly bigger and much cosier. I would be so excited and I would run up the big cobbled street to my Nana and Granda's door which was always open. That's the way it was in those days – everyone had an open door.

All the way you could smell the cooking of lunch as everybody cooked Sunday dinners in those days. The smell was gorgeous. I would run up the long curved staircase to the kitchen shouting "Nana, Granda" and when I reached the kitchen door I opened it and there would be my Granda waiting for us, sitting in his big armchair by the fire. He was a tall thick-set man with short lily-white hair. He was a heavy cripple and wore big, black, fat boots tied with laces and he walked with two walking sticks. He certainly wasn't a quiet man. He had a deep loud voice and a dirty laugh but his bark was always worse than his bite. He would say to each of us "hiya kidda" and lift us up one at a time, and sit us on his knee where he would give us a hug, kiss and a silver sixpence. I always felt rich on that day. A sixpence was a lot of money in those days and you could buy many sweets with it.

My nana would always be in the scullery cooking the Sunday dinner. We always had chicken and she would leave it to cool on the tray lying on top of the bench. The smell was absolutely gorgeous and there would always be some small pieces of chicken that had broken away and were floating amongst the juices in the tray. I couldn't resist pinching some of the small pieces and I would quickly put them in my mouth hoping nobody would notice, but you couldn't get away with anything when my nana was around. She may have been blind but she knew every move you made and everything you did. My nana always caught me out.

"Nana, how did you know what I was doing if you can't see me?"

She would always laugh and say, "Remember I have got eyes in the back of my head."

I really did begin to think she had eyes in the back of her head and I used to sometimes stare to try and see where they were and to see if they would move or blink. It's funny the things you believe that people say, when you're a child.

My nana was medium height and build, and had a lovely head of grey hair. She wore glasses that were like thick bottle tops, the same as my great aunt Hannah, her sister, who was also blind. It seems silly that they were given these horrible thick glasses to wear, which they couldn't even see out of anyway – how stupid is that? Maybe that was just something they did in those days, I don't know. When she smiled her whole face lit up. I absolutely loved and adored her.

There was a long sideboard in their room and a square table where she used to have her clippie mat. She used to have pieces of rags and I would be fascinated watching her putting them into the clippie mat. I was amazed at the different patterns she made.

My Dad was a crane operator. He worked away through the week and came home at weekends. I loved my dad; he was tall, slim, dark and handsome – well I thought he was anyway. He would always take us out somewhere like Leazes Park which was next to St James' football ground in Newcastle, which was just down the road from where I lived. He sometimes took us to the pictures where we had to wear those 3D glasses and, on a rare occasion, to a Chinese restaurant in Chinatown which was a special treat. I loved it; it was always great fun.

I also liked going to the wash house with my mam. She would put all the clothes into bags, put them into a pram and off we would go. I suppose many people today would find it a chore and quite boring going along to the launderette. In those days it was so different as very few had washing machines and if you had one, you must've been rich. Most of the women went along to the wash house. They were huge places, much different from the laundrettes today. They had great big top loader washing machines and spin dryers – and what a racket they made when they spun. It was like a great big whistling sound, and when many of them were spinning at the same time it used to hurt my ears. There were great big white sinks with wooden benches where many of the women would be washing and scrubbing their clothes by hand and everyone would have their pinnies and turbans on. It was hard work but everyone seemed to be enjoying themselves; they would be singing, laughing, carrying on and telling jokes and catching up with the weekly gossip. I suppose many of them classed it a great day out. I know my mam always did.

I remember going in my Auntie Florrie's tin bath. She would be boiling pans and kettles of water to fill it up and would put it in front of the fire and would put the old fashioned clothes horse around with blankets and towels on them so no one could see in – it was great fun. I could lie and stretch myself out and it was certainly much better than sitting cramped up in a sink, or standing in a dish of water like my mam had to do with us as we were not fortunate enough to have a tin bath, and the same bath water was used for everyone in the family. You thought nothing of it. That's just the way it was in those days.

I was very close to my Auntie Florrie and spent a lot of time with her, especially when my cousin Kim was born. I can remember from a very young age the amount of times my Auntie Florrie had to keep coming upstairs and putting us back into bed because of the noise we were making. Sometimes we would even go downstairs and be playing in the backyard with virtually no clothes on when it was raining. Apparently that was simply because my mam was never there as she would be out boozing every night down at the Gunners Club which was a pub at the bottom of the back lane where we lived. This happened when my dad was working away. As young as I was I will never forget the day when my dad arrived home unexpectedly from work. We were all having great fun crawling down the stairs head first to see who could get to the bottom the quickest. My dad went absolutely ballistic when he realised my mam wasn't there. We had been left on our own, but he knew exactly where she would be – 'the Gunners Club'. I don't know if he physically dragged her out of the Gunners Club but I can remember him pulling her by her arms through the back yard and up the stairs and into the kitchen.

There was a terrific blazing row. We were all huddled together, crying; it was awful. I hated to hear them arguing like that. There was no one who liked a drink more than my dad did but he would never go out leaving us on our own. I had just turned seven years old and went to Snow Street School in Newcastle. I was a happy little girl and loved living in Villa Place with my family and friends; I felt secure and safe.

Late one afternoon just as school was about to finish I didn't realise that my life was about to be shattered and turned inside out and upside down. There was a knock at the classroom door. I was in

Mrs Bow's class – she was lovely, an older teacher with grey hair tied up in a bun and she wore glasses. I looked towards the door when Mrs Bow went to open it and was surprised to see my mam there because she never took me to school and certainly never came to pick me up. I wondered why she was here. Mrs Bow and my mam were talking but I couldn't hear what they were saying. We were all sitting on the floor as Miss was telling us a story. Mrs Bow came over and gently took my hand and stood me in front of the class and said to them all, "Christine is leaving the school as from today and won't be coming back anymore as she is moving away."

I could hardly believe what I was hearing, because nobody had mentioned anything like that to me. Mrs Bow asked the class to say goodbye to me and when I heard my friends say that, as young as I was, I was absolutely devastated and began to cry. Mrs Bow quickly picked me up and I flung my arms around her neck and wrapped my legs around her waist.

She said, "Don't cry, Christine. We will all miss you but wherever you may go you will make new friends."

Once she said that it made me feel even worse. My cries became louder and louder. My mam was trying to pull me off Mrs Bow who was trying to put me down on the floor. I wasn't having any of it. I just wouldn't let go and clung on for grim death. By this time even some of the children were crying. Nobody could console me. I remember crying and sobbing all the way home and I will never forget that day as long as I live.

When I arrived home at Back Villa Place there was my twin brother John and my sister Jacqueline standing in the backyard and then I noticed that everything was packed up and ready to leave. We were moving to Heaton, which is another part of Newcastle but much further away from where we were now.

When we arrived at our new home what I didn't realise was that my mam had left my dad and that we were going to live with a new family and a new father. When I met this tall, slim man with thick, black, wavy hair, I knew I had met him before, once at his work when my mam stopped to talk to him and twice at our home when she introduced him as Uncle Bob. My thoughts were: I don't want to live in this place with these strangers whom I hadn't even met – because that is exactly what they were, 'strangers' – and I certainly didn't want a new dad – I already had one. All I wanted was to go back home where I belonged, but I knew that wasn't going to happen.

It was a four bedroomed terraced house with a lounge, sitting room and separate kitchen with a bathroom and toilet, large gardens to the front and a yard at the rear with a shed and a black Wolsey car to play in. The whole area was lovely. There were many large houses which all had beautiful gardens. Everywhere you looked there were trees and there were still some cobbled back lanes and a long cobbled street that led down to the river where we lived. It really was very pretty, far from what I was used to.

As we went into the house, I wasn't looking forward to meeting my new brothers and sister, but when we got together it wasn't as bad as I thought it was going to be. Gina was the oldest, she was sixteen; Gordon twelve, Leicester eight and Robin four. They were all full of fun and very friendly, and made us feel welcome. I always thought of Gina as a woman rather than a girl as she looked so grown up. She was also very quiet and rarely spoke at all.

Looking back it must have been harder for Gina than it was for us as she was older and more aware of what was going on. She was the one who had been left to take care of the children and her father. She was running the home as her mother had left them approximately eighteen months prior. Now she was faced with intruders moving in and another woman would take over her role as 'mother' and be head of the household. How dreadful it must have been for her.

After a while I began to settle in with my new brothers, but Gina played a very low key. I was still very shy and withdrawn from my Uncle Bob and sometimes found it difficult to speak to him. I missed my dad and grandparents terribly, and also my Aunt Florrie and Uncle Gordon and all my friends at Villa Place. I didn't know if I was going to see them again. I would quietly cry myself to sleep night after night just thinking about them and hoping no one would hear me in case I got wrong off my mam, as I knew I wasn't to talk about my dad of Villa Place. That was so hard to do. I can't even begin to explain the pain I was feeling; it was heart rending, 'awful'. I never had a chance to say goodbye to anyone, but from an adult's point of view we are just children and they forget we also have thoughts and feelings. No matter how young we may be we understand more than they give us credit for. They should remember that we are the innocent ones dragged into this horrible bloody mess through no fault of our own.

We, as adults, and parents, can learn so much from our children. We need to sit down and communicate with our children to avoid them becoming unhappy. Some may end up disturbed and they might just end up going down the wrong path. This is usually a cry for help.

My new grandparents lived in a house adjoining our back garden. I could jump down off the wall and be in their drive. Their garden and house were beautiful. They even had a television the same as my Uncle Bob's. I had never seen or heard of a television before and I was totally amazed by it. I just remember listening to the wireless at my Nana and Granda Gardener's house. I would be waiting for the one o'clock Billy Cotton Band Show and I would be standing with my ear glued to the radio waiting for the shout 'wakey wakey'. Music and jokes would follow. For me, that was the best part of the day on a Sunday, listening to the radio while eating your Sunday dinner with your grandparents and family around you.

I remember walking into my Nana and Granda Hall's front room for the first time. It was breathtaking. It was like walking into fairyland as the sun shone through the window. Everything was bright, sparkly and glittering. I had never seen so many beautiful things. There was china, clocks, glass, crystal and many ornaments. I used to spend hours in there just looking at everything. I had never seen anything like it before.

My Granda Hall also had a car; I thought they must be very rich. I didn't know anyone who had a car, except my Uncle Gordon who worked for Pepsi Cola. He had one of their vans for work, and on a very rare occasion, which was a special treat, he would let us sit in the back of the van and take us for a ride up the street. It was great. My Granda Hall would sometimes take us out for a drive in the car. I couldn't believe I was going into a real car. I was so excited and I would be like the Queen sitting in the back of the car and waving to everyone as I passed them. I felt so important – it was magical.

That was many years ago, and I am not that little girl anymore. I am sixteen years of age and lying flat on my back in a hospital bed with cot sides up. *How the hell has it come to this?*

Chapter 3

Just over three weeks ago I was working in Boots the Chemist. The next thing I know I am in the Queen Elizabeth Hospital having my stomach pumped, lying in a flaming straightjacket because they thought I had taken a bloody overdose. Then I was put into that horrible old army ward with all those very sick elderly people being treated like a second class citizen by that horrible doctor, because he thought I was a junkie and off my bloody trolley. Then they decided to shove me into a frigging nut house. I was terrified and thought I'd never get out. I was one of the lucky ones because of one woman doctor who worked there at that particular time. I was treated like an animal, being dragged across the floor and flung into a padded cell; I was just a nobody as nobody seemed to care.

Now here I am in the Newcastle General Hospital lying paralysed from the chest down. I am only able to move my arms and head. What on earth has happened to me this time? Something has obviously gone terribly wrong. How come this elderly lady came in this morning and spoke to me? She was up and about and had the same operation as myself. She was much older than I was, so why wasn't I walking about too?

I really thought I was going to get well looked after and cared for in this hospital but instead I felt totally abandoned by everyone including my mam – she wasn't even here and should have been. I needed someone to speak for me as there were many questions I wanted to ask but didn't quite know where to start. My mam was at home looking after my younger brothers and sister – my Dad Hall could have looked after them, there was no excuse. I needed her here and for that one important day her place should have been here with me to fight my corner, to ask the many questions that needed to be asked. I wasn't very forthcoming or had much confidence in myself in those days – after all I was still only young – but I knew I had to take the 'bull by the horns' and I thought that the next doctor or nurse who comes in through that door, I must ask them something. Not long afterwards a nurse and doctor came in together, but before they could ask how I was I immediately spoke out and asked, "What on earth has happened to me? What have they done?"

The nurse went on to say, "Remember how you were transferred from St Mary's so we could do some deep head X-rays on you? That is what has been done."

I replied: "How am I lying here like this when an elderly patient came in this morning just to say hello – she had had the same operation as me yesterday and is now up and walking about. How come I'm not?"

They said I had also had a lumbar puncture done. When I asked "what do you mean by that?" they began to explain. However, the terminology and the medical words they used were too difficult for me to grasp and to understand.

"I was told that it was a simple and straightforward operation that would only take an hour. I would be fine afterwards and put straight back on the ward. Look at me now: here I am lying paralysed almost from the neck down, I can't feel my body or even move. My eyes are still hurting and when the light is shining it feels as if they are being burnt. Nobody explained that any of this would happen to me – surely something must have gone wrong here..."

To which they replied: "Christine, every operation is different but unfortunately there were some complications and we had to do the operation again."

I asked, "What kind of complications do you mean?" – which they did not fully explain. All they kept saying was that there are sometimes complications during operations; unfortunately this was one of them.

Apparently the one hour operation had eventually turned into four and a half hours. I wasn't convinced that they were telling me the whole truth at the time and that there was more to it than meets the eye simply because of the way they spoke; everything was just 'matter of fact'. They were so blasé about everything and when I looked at their faces there was no emotion as though they weren't even bothered. To them I was just another patient but of course they weren't the ones that were lying here. I then commented on my neck – I could feel there was something hanging down and wondered what it was. They explained that was where I was operated on.

"You have four puncture marks on your neck – that was where they had injected the fluid to go around your head to see if you had any brain tumours and what you can feel is just the loose skin that is hanging."

The doctor then reached over and pulled the loose skin off which didn't hurt. He asked if I would like to see where the puncture marks were and I replied, "Yes, I would."

He then went away and came back with a small mirror but I made it quite clear to him that I only wanted to see the puncture marks and not my face as I knew it would be in a terrible state with bruising all over and I couldn't bear to look at myself as I was frightened.

As the doctor and nurse left the room another two nurses came in to turn me over on to my side as I had to be turned every four hours. They would put a pillow between my legs, one behind my back and one at my front. This gave me support and kept me secure. It was lunchtime and they had brought my dinner in to feed me and also to give me a drink. I had never seen anything so weird – it was like a little teapot with a long spout on it; it looked more like a watering can. It was sometimes very difficult to eat and drink due to the awkward position I was lying in. I had been dribbling all over the place and I felt like a small child again when they had to keep wiping my mouth.

After lunch I must have drifted off to sleep and when I woke up I was looking through the cot sides on my bed and I could see my mam sitting there. She could see that I was awake and made no attempt to speak to me and when I looked at her she looked as miserable as sin and totally fed up as if she couldn't wait to get away and go back home, but I knew that if it had been one of my other brothers or sisters she would have been full of chat and asking how they were. I only wanted a smile – that would have been enough for me, but she didn't even give me that.

They were long days lying in the hospital, especially being on a side ward, on your own, and unable to get up and walk about. I became terribly lonely and just wanted somebody to talk to. I hadn't seen my dad or brothers or sisters for weeks now since I'd been in hospital and my mam didn't come in very often to see me and sometimes I wondered why she even bothered – she had no conversation. Maybe it was out of guilt or duty but it certainly wasn't out of love.

I have heard many people say that when you become sixteen that the world is your oyster and that your whole life and future lies ahead of you. At that minute I was so unhappy and depressed, I didn't even know if I was going to walk again. My eyes were burning and becoming more sensitive to light that I had to wear dark glasses. I couldn't bear to think what might happen next. My life was just going from bad to worse and I didn't see a future for me. These last nine years since my mam left my dad had just been horrendous, one thing just seemed to happen after the other and sometimes I wondered when it was all going to come to an end.

Chapter 4

We had only lived at Heaton three months when my three new brothers were sent back to Leicester to go and live with their mother again. It was awful when we had to say goodbye to them as we all had grown closer together as brothers and sisters. For many years I had been led to believe that it was their mother who had sent for them and wanted them back again. It wasn't until the year 2000 that I found out the truth – that it was simply my mother who didn't want them anymore and had sent them packing on an almost fourteen hour bus journey back to Leicester on their own. How cruel is that?

On January 4th 1962 my Nana Gardner (my mam's mother) died. I was eight years old. I only wish my mam had sat me down and explained it in a nicer way about my nana's death as it would have helped me to cope with it a lot more instead of saying, she had just died and that I wouldn't be seeing her again. I absolutely worshipped and adored her as she was the one who loved and cared for me. She felt more like my mother.

I had never thought about dying before and from that day it just haunted me. In June 1962 we moved from Heaton as the house had to be sold. We went to live over the river in Gateshead at Redheugh Road. I was sad to leave Heaton as I had enjoyed living there and had made a lot of new friends. It wasn't as heart-rending as leaving Back Villa Place – at least I had a chance to say goodbye to everyone. I was looking forward to moving to Gateshead.

My mam and Uncle Bob had bought two flats; we were to live in the upstairs one with two large attics. It reminded me very much of Back Villa Place. We were going back to the long old cobbled streets, with an outdoor toilet, backyard, scullery, no bath and going back to standing in a dish to get washed down. I knew I was going to be happy here as it was very much like the place where I had been born and brought up. I became very close to my Uncle Bob and grew to love him and began to call him Dad. I settled in very well at Redheugh Road and began to make lots of new friends. There were lots of boys who lived there and they used to play football and cricket in the street and would let me join in the games and before I knew it I became a right little tomboy and one of the lads. We would build bogies and knock on the neighbour's doors and ask if they had any old spare wood or old pram wheels. Everyone went around in gangs, roller skating or playing with their top and whips. The streets would be full of children playing out. We would play 'knocky nine door', 'hide and seek', 'hit the can', 'tuggy' and 'conkers'.

In the weeks leading up to Guy Fawkes Night we would all be going round collecting wood. Everyone made a guy and we would all stand on street corners and outside shops asking for a penny for the guy so we could raise some money to buy some fireworks. We used to have bonfires in the streets in those days but you wouldn't be allowed to do that now. All the kids would come round from other streets to ours because we had a huge bonfire. The street would be lined with old furniture, armchairs and settees and we would all be sitting on them waiting for the jacket potatoes to finish cooking in the fire. It was a great way for people to get rid of their old and unwanted furniture as they didn't have the council or the environmental health to come and take them away, so they would wait for Guy Fawkes Night to get rid of them and burn them on the fire. Some of the parents would come out and join in the fun and they would set their fireworks off in the street for everyone to see. People were more neighbourly in those days.

Each year we had fantastic winters – it would snow for weeks and we'd all look forward to sledging but not everyone was fortunate enough to have a sledge so we would use anything we could find, such as a shovel, a sheet of polythene or a piece of plastic etc. We always had great fun. We used to make great big long slides that were almost the length of the street. They were lethal as they were like a sheet of glass which you could almost see your face in. We even made long slides on the pavements which were outside people's doors and when the neighbours came out they went flying on them. We would pretend that we hadn't seen what had happened and we'd laugh our heads off thinking it was a great big joke. They would shout and raise their fists at us, but when you're young like that you don't realise how dangerous it can be for others.

Many children in those days would do messages for the elderly to get their groceries at the corner shop. Well at least I know I did. Some gave you a penny and others maybe a pop or beer bottle. The shopkeeper would give us thre'pence for each bottle and we would buy sweets with the money. Those are the nice happy memories that I try to hold onto and remember. Most children were very innocent in those days – I know I was. I trusted everybody, especially my family and older people.

There was an old man who lived in the next street to us; everybody called him 'Grandad', even myself. He would always stand at the front door and watch us play in the street. He always appeared to wear the same clothes – a cap, a waistcoat with a checky shirt and reddish dark brown corduroy trousers. He always looked pleasant and used a walking stick to help him walk although his legs didn't appear to be bad. Sometimes he would ask me to go a message to the corner shop for him and I always did. His daughter and grandson used to visit him quite often and I would play with his grandson outside. He would be about five or six years old, and on a few occasions I had been invited to his daughter's house for tea.

Whenever Grandad asked me to go a message for him he would always bring his bag to the front door. When I came back from the shops he would still be standing there and I would just give him his bag of shopping. On this particular day Grandad said he couldn't find his bag and asked if I would come in to help him find it. Every week I went shopping for two elderly ladies who were housebound; I used to go into their house to get their bag for them so I thought nothing about going into Grandad's house for his. He stepped to the side of the doorway, pointed his arm down the corridor and invited me in.

"Just go straight down the corridor, Christine and into that bottom room on the right and I'll follow you."

I automatically walked down to the bottom of the corridor into the room and thought nothing of it. But what I hadn't realised was that Grandad had locked all the doors behind him. I was in the kitchen, the sideboard was to the right and a large kitchen table to the left and the scullery was facing me on the opposite side of the room.

When Grandad came into the room he went across to the opposite side of the kitchen table which was away from the door and sat down on a chair. He began to fumble for some money in his pocket and I immediately saw his so-called lost bag. He asked me to come over so he could give me the money and bag for the groceries. Unexpectedly he grabbed me so quickly and pulled me into his chest with one arm round my back and the other round my neck. He was so strong and held me tight; he terrified me. I couldn't move or breathe. He began to kiss me and put his tongue in my mouth – it was that horrible I felt sick.

Suddenly someone knocked loudly on the front door. Grandad jumped as he got a fright and let go of me so I tried to turn and run but unfortunately he grabbed me once again. Then there was another loud knock and again he let go with fright and this time I was able to kick him and run away. He may have been old and had a bit of a gammy leg but I have never seen anyone move so fast. I didn't even manage to get halfway round the table when he came after me like a raving lunatic.

I was absolutely terrified. I don't know if he hit me or pushed me but I ended up on the floor and just missed hitting my head on the sideboard. The next minute he was on top of me trying to rip my blouse off. Even to this day I honestly don't know how I managed to get away alive from that horrible man. I strongly believe that if the person had not continued to knock at the front door for what seemed like forever things may have turned out very differently indeed.

The ordeal was horrendous and my mind was scarred terribly, and it still lives with me today after all these years. Although the police were involved I never knew what happened to the man and my mam made it quite clear that it was never to be spoken of again. It was alright my mam saying that, but what about me? It didn't happen to her and I needed to talk to someone about it who would listen and understand how I was feeling. My mam probably thought that because I was only ten years old it didn't really matter and that I'd be fine and would have forgotten all about it in a few days. It would be as if nothing had ever happened.

I think sometimes adults just don't understand and think that because we are young we accept everything that is thrown our way, whatever it may be. I may have only been ten years old but I have memories, thoughts and feelings just like anybody else including grown-ups.

At the minute I am feeling so unhappy and finding it very hard to accept everything that has happened to me over the last three and a half years. I can't stop crying and thinking about my Dad Pattinson. I miss you, Dad, I loved you so much and I will never forget you. I don't even know where you are, but I promise one day I will find you, no matter how long it takes me I know I will find you one day. My Nana Gardner has left me; I can't bear it. Why did you have to die and leave me like this on my own? She was the one who loved me and felt like my mother.

I can't stop thinking about dying now, it's horrible. It haunts me; it's like a disease – it festers and never seems to go away. I'm having nightmares about that horrible man I called Grandad: his face is on top of mine, I'm suffocating, I can't breathe. I'm trying to get away and I don't think I'm going to make it to the front door. I feel I am not going to get out of here alive. Then I wake up.

I attended Redheugh Infants and Junior School which was an all-girls school but I was finding it very difficult to concentrate on my work. I was never a bright or clever child anyway and my work was beginning to slip further and further behind. I felt my mind was under so much pressure it was buzzing, and it upset me when my mam kept telling me how thick and stupid I was that I truly began to believe it. I lost confidence in myself and could no longer cope with my work. I began to cheat by copying other people's books who sat next to me and hoped nobody would find out.

I wanted my mam to see that I was clever, I wanted her to be proud of me, but unfortunately I was caught. The teacher brought me to the front of the class and told everybody what I had done. I wasn't proud of myself as I knew I'd done wrong. The teacher then put a dunce's hat on top of my head and I was told to go and stand in the corner and face the wall. The whole class laughed at me. That's all I feel I am to everyone: one big joke. Just a stupid little girl who is supposed to have no feelings and because I'm young, grown-ups think that they can just use and abuse me in any way they feel fit and I just have to stand there and take it all.

I've just turned eleven and I'm feeling much worse. I don't know what's wrong with me. I'm beginning to pass out at school. Sometimes my hands begin to shake; I try to stop them but I can't – they seem as if they're out of control. My mind is sometimes so mixed up that I can't even think straight and my mam is now taking me to see a doctor who has given me some tablets but I don't know why or what I'm taking them for. Sometimes I get so fed up with life I feel worthless, a nobody, only my mam's skivvy. If it wasn't cleaning she had me doing it would be ironing; if it wasn't ironing it would be shopping or babysitting for my little brother and sister when my mam and dad went out to the bingo or to the pub for a drink.

I'll be twelve shortly and we've all just been given the devastating news: Redheugh Road and many of the other streets in the area are to be pulled down to make way for new development. I was totally gutted. I never thought for one minute that we would ever move again. Although there had been many upsets, I liked living here as I had made so many good friends and enjoyed very much playing and being with them. I could hardly face or believe that once again I was having to leave all my friends behind knowing I would never see them again. Apparently the council was already building a new housing estate to accommodate most of the people from our area. It was known as Lindhurst estate but it wasn't quite finished yet. My dad worked on the Team Valley Trading Estate which was roughly two and a half miles away from where we lived. Jackie, John and I went to Hill Head Secondary Modern School which was half a mile further up the road from my dad's work in a little place called Lobley Hill. My mam and dad put in for a council house there. We were very lucky and were quickly offered a four bedroomed semi-detached house.

We left Redheugh Road the first week of January 1966 to go and live at our new home. We were one of the first families to leave Redheugh Road. It was terrible saying goodbye to some of our neighbours and many of my friends came to see me off. As I hugged each one of them and said goodbye for the last time we were all in tears. It was awful; I hated it. None of my friends knew exactly where they were moving to. Nothing was quite the same after leaving Redheugh Road.

Chapter 5

Lobley Hill was a lovely area with big houses and gardens; ours was huge. It was good to have an indoor toilet and especially a bathroom. We even had an outdoor wash house. The neighbours were friendly and I had made lots of new friends. The main problem I'm facing at the moment though is going to Hill Head School which consists of two buildings, one for the boys and one for the girls. I am being bullied terribly by some of the girls at our school. Every morning when I get up for school I feel physically sick and think I am going to throw up. This is before I even get there. I never knew from one day to the next what they were going to do to me. How could children be so malicious and cruel? I wasn't the only one who was bullied – there were plenty others. But there was one particular girl who just wouldn't leave me alone. She had even threatened to kill me on quite a few occasions, especially if I told my mam or anyone else about the things she said and did to me. I was terrified of her. I always took her punishment and did everything she said. I believed every word and thought she would carry out her threats without hesitation. She was a horrible, wicked and sadistic person.

I am now sixteen. Over these last four years I have tried to put my traumas and past behind me, but it is so hard to do. I would put on a brave face and pretend that I was always happy, so nobody thought anything was wrong. I thought I was coping and everything was alright; nobody saw the signs (not even me), because I was too young to understand. I didn't realise how badly my mind was affected and I wasn't well – but how did other people not notice? How did my mam not know that I wasn't well? No wonder I became ill and ended up in hospital, because of what that bastard of a grandad did to me and also the mental abuse I suffered. They all totally screwed and messed my mind up. I ended up having a breakdown and became a severe epileptic at the same time.

Apparently epilepsy runs in the family. Just my luck to bloody well have it.

Chapter 6

So here I am lying in a hospital bed paralyzed from the chest down, only able to move my head and arms. I can't bear the thought that I might never walk again and still nobody has convinced me yet that I will. I've been in Newcastle General Hospital for a week now and I expressed to a nurse one morning that I was feeling very lonely in this room on my own.

"I can soon fix that," she said. Within no time my bed was moved to a larger ward. It was so good to be amongst other people and hear different conversations. A few days later when the doctors were doing their rounds they suggested that the back of my bed should be wound up slightly, "then you'll be able to see what's going on, Christine".

Well that certainly put a smile on my face. It was much better than lying flat and straining through the cot sides of the bed to see everyone. My thoughts were that I must be improving which made me feel much happier.

Another week has passed and I can hardly believe what has just happened! All of a sudden out of the blue I automatically sat up. The feeling was coming back into my body and legs. I began to shout out loudly for the nurses and kept repeating myself over and over again, probably with shock as well as excitement. Everyone around looked so startled; I suppose at first they were all wondering what was wrong.

You would have thought I had just won the pools but this was far better than that – it was the best I had felt in ages. Shortly afterwards the doctors came to examine me. I could see by the look on their faces that they were just as relieved and as happy as I was. However there was still no explanation given. I wasn't allowed to get out of bed until the following day when two nurses came in to get me up. I was so excited but at the same time I remember feeling very apprehensive.

When I first stood up I felt very light headed and off balance; my legs were so weak and wobbly, I felt hesitant and didn't quite know how to move them, so I just stood for a short while to get my mind and body focussed. The nurses took an arm each and off we went. They walked me out of the ward, down the corridor and back again. I was very slow at first and it was more like a shuffle than anything else, but it didn't matter. The most important thing was that I managed and done it. I was totally on cloud nine but what I didn't know was that there was another massive thunderstorm just about to happen very shortly.

Over the next couple of days the nurses took me on many short walks. I was now feeling more confident and already my legs were much stronger. The following morning I got out of bed and managed to walk on my own. I took my time and was very careful. What a feeling it was! I went on many walks that day. I was so happy and I was really enjoying myself. It certainly helped me to appreciate what I now have after being paralyzed and lying in bed for those two and a half weeks. It is so easy to take so many things for granted.

That same day, in the evening, a nurse came to tell me that there was a John Wayne film on TV in the day room and that I might like to go and watch it. I quite liked John Wayne but I hadn't seen many of his films and I thought *why not?* It was quite a small, dowdy room with a few armchairs and a coffee table. There was no one else there but me. *Good,* I thought, *I can have the whole room to myself.* In about fifteen minutes' time though, once again my life is about to change traumatically.

All of a sudden, within a flash, everything was in darkness and I initially thought there had been a power-cut. At the time it didn't dawn on me that the TV was still on; my main concern was why had all the lights gone out. I was pleased that the chair I was sitting in was right next to the door leading into the corridor so at least I knew where I was and couldn't get lost. As I turned and looked down either side of the corridor I couldn't see a thing in front of me. I thought nobody will be able to see where they're going because of this power cut, as there were no windows in the corridor because they were all side cubicles on either side. *But where is everyone? And why is it so quiet?*

I realised that all the patients would probably be asleep in bed as time was getting on and it was well after ten o'clock. I expected to hear more chit chat and fuss come from the nurses about the problem that was going on. I then decided to try and find my way back to the ward. The next thing I know, bang, I had walked straight into a wall. I didn't hurt myself. I was more shocked than anything else. It wasn't until then, and only then, that I realised something was seriously wrong.

I began to panic and became paranoid about being in the dark. My brain seemed to shoot into auto-pilot. Horrible thoughts seemed to be flashing through my mind at high speed. Eventually I became hysterical, shouting and screaming at high pitch for the nurses. The nurses were furious with me – after all it was late at night and I remember as they pulled and shoved me back into bed they gave me a right dressing-down. And who could have blamed them? They had every right because within a matter of seconds I had the whole place in an uproar.

When I lay down I knew it was my sight that had gone and not the lights as I had first thought. I never knew that anything like this could happen so quickly. I felt totally ashamed of myself because I knew I had woken and upset many very sick patients. There were two other boys just a few years older than I was and they were both blind, immobile and dying from a brain tumour. I had yet to hear them complain. There was no excuse at all for my behaviour and selfishness that night. I only wish the nurses had taken the time to try and understand what I was saying to them.

So nobody knew of my predicament until the following morning when the nurses came to wake me up. They showed very little concern when I told them. It was as if it was an everyday thing that happened – maybe it was because I was on a neurology ward. But it didn't make me feel any better. Shortly afterwards the doctors came to examine my eyes and to hear what had happened. They explained there could be a number of reasons as to why I had lost my sight – firstly the new medication I was taking for epilepsy and also because of the hereditary of blindness through the family or because of the several knocks I had received recently to my head during fits and seizures.

The doctors remarked that there was nothing more they could say or do and would be referring me to see an eye specialist in the hospital very shortly. I was then told because I was up and about they felt I was now well enough to be transferred back to St Mary's at Stannington where I would be discharged and sent home. The doctors then stood up and walked out of the ward. I was totally gutted at their 'couldn't care less' attitude. There was very little compassion in those days, no counselling, no back-up; you just had to get on with it! I felt as if I had just been hung, drawn and quartered. All the stuffing had been knocked out of me. I wasn't looking forward to going back to Stannington even if it was only for a few days. I absolutely hated it there.

Once again I was feeling rock bottom; my morale was low. I wanted to cry but I couldn't even do that! It wouldn't have made any difference anyway – you certainly wouldn't have got any sympathy. Nobody seemed to care. They were as hard as nails. Some of the nurses and doctors were okay but others were horrors.

I feel I have nothing to look forward to. I don't know if I'll ever see again. Although I have been in hospital for seven weeks my mam has only been in to see me on the odd occasion. She must have fallen out with my Auntie Florrie again and hasn't told her where I am because I know she would have come in to see me if she knew. They were always falling out as my Auntie Florrie was very outspoken and would tell my mam some home truths about herself and her behaviour which she never liked to hear. Even my dad, brothers and sisters haven't been in to see me, due to the fact that my mam probably wouldn't have allowed it. I've really missed them. I'm even anxious about going home because I don't know what response I'm going to get from my family and neighbours as I don't know what my mam has told them.

Chapter 7

Two days later I was transferred from Newcastle General Hospital
to St Mary's psychiatric at Stannington. When I arrived there
the doctor whom I had seen previously came to see me and he
explained that he'd received news from Newcastle General Hospital
that I was to be discharged from Stannington the following day.
The doctor asked if I would stay a few extra days as they would like
to do more tests and assessments on me. "No way!" I replied.

"Why? So you can put me back in that bloody horrible padded
cell again when you feel like it! There is no way I am staying here a
minute longer than I have to."

He explained how important it was for me to have these tests
and assessments done to help towards their work. I was very hesitant
and must have been stupid to have agreed but I felt as if they had
me pinned into a corner and that there was no way out and I
couldn't refuse.

"Two days," I replied, "and not one minute longer, and I mean
not one minute more."

I have no recollection of the last days I spent in Stannington or
even being discharged from there. For all I know they could have
kept me there much longer. I suppose I'll never know what really
happened. The only thing I do remember was feeling something
being pushed against my lips which woke me up. I could hear
people laughing and shouting in the background. I recognised
their voices – it was my brothers and sisters. It was then I realised I
was lying in my own bed at home and it was my mam trying to put
tablets into my mouth while I was still lying down and half asleep. I
could feel them melting in my mouth and they tasted horrible. My
mouth was as dry as sticks. She would then leave the room without

even giving me a glass of water to wash them down with. No wonder I eventually lost most of my teeth as they dropped out and I had to get false ones. I didn't have the energy to sit up or even speak as I was literally doped up to the eyeballs with medication. My Auntie Florrie used to come over and she told me how my mam used to brag to her about how I slept all day and every day. "I just go up and shove the tablets in her mouth when they're due and leave her there and come back downstairs."

My Auntie Florrie told me much later how upset and disgusted she was about the way I was being treated by my mam. "I wanted to come upstairs to see you but I couldn't bring myself to do it as I couldn't bear to see the state you were in."

My Auntie Florrie wanted to tell my mam exactly what she thought about her and to give her a piece of her mind. She would have normally, without hesitation, but on this occasion she thought it was best to keep her tongue between her teeth. Knowing my Auntie Florrie, it must have been hard for her to do so because they would have fallen out again and she didn't want that as she knew that my mam wouldn't allow her to have any contact with me at all. It took a few weeks before my body adjusted to the medication and I was able to stay up for a few hours. I remember it felt so good to have a wash and brush my teeth because I was literally stinking after all that time in bed.

During that time my Auntie Florrie approached my mam to ask if I could go over for a couple of weeks to stay with her and the family because she knew how much my mam had neglected me as I had almost lost three and a half stone. All my muscle tone had gone and I was virtually unable to walk because my feet were so sore and swollen that I had to crawl around on my hands and knees. I was a total wreck. It was very hard at first trying to cope and adapt without being able to see. I would be bumping into everything. Sometimes I hadn't a clue where I was. I hated it and lost all my confidence and thought I would never be able to do anything on my own again.

My Aunt Florrie and Uncle Gordon came to pick me up in their car and took me to their house. I was so excited that I couldn't wait to get away. I was so pleased because I always enjoyed going over there but I felt really embarrassed about my Uncle Gordon having to carry me to the car.

Altogether I stayed with my Aunt Florrie for just over three weeks and it did me the world of good being there. She got me back on my feet, I gained weight and felt much stronger and more confident in myself. The only downfall for me was having to go back home.

The days were long and lonely; my younger brothers and sister were at school, my twin brother was at work and my other two sisters were up away and married. I felt uncomfortable sitting downstairs. My mam and dad would be pottering around doing some chores. They never spoke to me and treated me as if I was invisible. The behaviour was unusual for my dad because he was a lovely man and we got on well but it was my mam who wore the trousers in the house. He wouldn't have dared to step out of line or he would have been in serious trouble.

Even my friends had disappeared – not one of them called to see how I was. It's strange when something goes wrong in your life; no one seems to care – well, that's how it looked at the time. It made me feel angry and frustrated I felt isolated from everyone and didn't feel part of the family anymore. I wanted to talk to someone so I could express how I was feeling and to go for a walk and have some fun and feel normal again, but instead I was made to feel like a frigging freak.

I spent most days in my bedroom listening to the radio; it was the only place where I felt safe and could be myself. I would kick and punch the walls, swear and shout as much as I liked and no one would know or hear me as my bedroom was above the alleyway and wash house. I was so unhappy. All I seemed to do was cry and feel sorry for myself. I longed to see my Aunt Florrie again but my mam and her had fallen out so all contact was stopped between the two families. I began to hate everybody including God – to me he was the biggest bastard of them all and I blamed him for everything. If it hadn't been for him I wouldn't have been born, and how I wished I hadn't.

There were times I just wanted to curl up and die and prayed I wouldn't wake up in the morning. But that would have been the easy way out. One evening as I went to the bathroom I could hear everyone laughing and giggling downstairs. It sounded as if they were all having a whale of a time. I was jealous and green with envy. I went back to my room, left the door ajar and opened a big bag of salted peanuts which were my favourites and also my mam's.

I could still hear them and my blood was beginning to boil. I went downstairs and flung the sitting room door open, but still holding my bag of peanuts. Suddenly there was a deadly silence. I bet they nearly shit themselves, wondering what I was going to do. "What's the matter? Have I interrupted something?" I said. "Don't let me stop your fun – I'm pleased someone's enjoying themselves because I'm fucking well not. You've all forgotten about me. I'm like a fucking prisoner in this house and I hate it here. I want to go out somewhere. Nobody's even taken me for a walk yet, yeah a walk, a fucking simple walk – that's all I'm asking for... or is that too much to ask anyone to do?"

I then walked further into the room. "You like salted peanuts, mam? Here! Have some of mine," I said. I turned the bag upside down and poured them all over the floor and then said, "Now you can come and pick them up and grovel all over the floor like I had to and see how you fucking well like it. You're nothing but a bastard and I hate you."

I turned and walked back out of the room. No one uttered a word. I suppose I left them all in a state of shock. I went back up to my bedroom and began to shake like a leaf. I couldn't believe what I had just done I wouldn't normally speak to anyone like that and especially not to my parents. I always treated them with the greatest of respect no matter what they had said or done. I was horrified at the foul language I had used and was totally ashamed and disgusted with myself. I went back downstairs and apologized for the way I had behaved.

No matter what walk of life we may come from sometimes you can only take so much before you snap. It may have been upsetting and unpleasant but it certainly did the trick and things began to change for the better.

I'm feeling much happier now. My mam and dad have started taking me out with them once a fortnight to the Rose Shamrock and Thistle, which is a small country pub just a couple of miles from where we live. My parents had been going there for some time; they were both very popular and my mam was on the darts team. It felt so good to be out of the house and to be amongst other people. It was a lovely little pub, everyone was so friendly and made me feel welcome. They were all a lot older than I was but it didn't matter – I got on well with everyone. We talked, laughed and told jokes. It was brilliant; they made me feel so happy and made a fuss of me and gave me a lot of attention which was just what I needed.

I enjoyed every minute and soaked up all the atmosphere. It was a very special place filled with very special people. I want to say thank you to you my friends wherever you may be today, how much you all played a part in saving my life and sanity. I have not forgotten any of you. I still think of you all today and always will. You have my eternal gratitude and love.

Chapter 8

Over a year has passed and I am much happier now. My mam's been great. I only hope and pray it will last as it is the closest I have ever felt to her, but my dad was also a wonderful man whom I adored and loved to bits. My mam has went and bought me lots of new clothes including hot pants – apparently they're all the rage at the minute.

I was registered blind in 1971 and had to attend Newcastle General eye infirmary. My older sister Gina who used to live abroad was now back home, so my mam and Gina used to take turns in accompanying me to the Newcastle eye infirmary.

Mr Howard was my consultant. He was a tall, elderly man, probably not far off retiring age – what a lovely person he was. He would make me laugh as soon as I walked in the room. "Hello my little sweetie pie," he would say, "come and sit over here beside me and let me look into those beautiful eyes of yours." He made me feel at ease immediately.

The eye department was a very large place and no matter whenever you went in it was always full to the brim with patients. Sometimes they even ran out of seats and many would have to stand. I would be there for hours, sometimes even all day, especially if I were brought in by ambulance. There were people of all ages from the very elderly down to the young and babies in arms. Although it could be very boring sitting here for the best part of the day it gave me time to stop and think of others, more so about the young children and babies who were also blind. It gave me a lot of food for thought when I went home. It made me realise that I wasn't the only blind person in the world and it was about time I got my act together and pulled my socks up and stopped crying and feeling sorry for myself. It is so easy to fall into self pity and keep asking yourself why me? I was allocated a social worker for the blind and also a B.P.R.O. (a blind person's resettlement officer) – both came to visit me on a regular basis to help build my confidence and to advise me how to use my new white cane.

"I don't want it!" I couldn't bear the thought of using one. Mr Gray, who was my B.P.R.O., replied, "It is a must because you need it, and it would be a great help for you to be able to find your way about. I've been blind for years, Christine, and I would never have managed without my white cane – it goes everywhere with me and you should never be ashamed of using it."

He could still tell that I wasn't totally convinced. "Christine," he said, "think of your white cane as a pair of eyes: your eyes reflect and send impulses to your brain telling you what's out there. Your cane will work in exactly the same way and it will help you to stop walking into objects by touching them first. When using your cane the sounds will change so you know whether you are passing a wall, gate, fence or coming to the end of a street and also the end and beginning of kerbs and much more. Do you know that we all have five senses and we hardly ever use them? Now you're going to have to learn how to develop them even further. Your ears will tell you everything that is happening around you and even where you are. Your nose will pick up what shops you're coming up to and some that you've even passed and also don't forget about your hands and feet because they can tell you many things. But the most important thing is that you have to believe in yourself. Have lots of confidence, always use your common sense and remember you can train your brain to do anything you want it to do. And do you know what? The world can be your oyster – don't let anyone tell you any different or destroy your morale."

He was a very knowledgeable and wise old man; he taught me so much.

Chapter 9

It is January 1972 and I have just turned eighteen. I've just had another visit from Mr Gray and he suggested that it would be good for me to go away to a rehabilitation centre for the blind and partially sighted in Fife where I would receive intense mobility training.

"No thanks," I replied, "I'm quite happy just to stay here."

He advised me to give it a lot of thought before I made my decision as "the vacancies for trainees fill up quickly and if you agree to go it will be happening on the 10th of April and you will be returning back home in the middle of July."

"Three months!" I said. "There's no way I'm going anywhere for three months."

"Look, I'll be back at the beginning of February to hear your decision and I hope it will be the right one."

As far as I was concerned my decision was made anyway: no way hosay. Sure enough he was back at the beginning of February as promised. I had given it a lot of thought and my conclusion was there was no way that I wanted to go away and spend three months with a load of blind people.

"Why not?" he asked.

"Well, first of all I have never been away from home before and especially on my own in a strange place, I'll never be able to manage or find my way about. It's bad enough being in a room filled with strangers but a room filled with blind people I can't bear the thought of it."

"Christine, you have told me many times how lonely it can be and wished you had some friends the same age as yourself to talk to. This will be the greatest opportunity you will ever get. I've been in touch with Fife and found out that there are some young people like yourself going in April. I believe by going there it will be the making of you – it's just what you need and it will do you the world of good. You will learn so much and they will teach you many different things there. It really is a wonderful place and you never know – when you come back you might teach me a thing or two!" He laughed. "Go on, what do you say?"

I felt more reassured and happier this time when he spoke to me about it.

"I still don't know, I'll have to think about it," I said. "I don't want to feel that I'm being bullied and pressured into something that I might regret. To me it's a very big decision and I want to make sure I make the right one."

"Okay, I can only give you another two weeks to make your decision as the centre has to know five to six weeks in advance if you're going."

I eventually made my decision to go. Mr Gray was thrilled. I was now quite excited myself but still a little anxious and hoped I had made the right decision. I was looking forward to making new friends. I was lonely, but most of all I was hoping I would find a companion. I've never seriously thought about going out with boys and having a boyfriend because as a child I was a tomboy always playing football and cricket with the lads, but that was just kids' stuff. This time it was different – I didn't want to be on my own for the rest of my life and I couldn't imagine any sighted boy wanting to get serious with someone who was blind. The only chance I'll probably ever have is to meet someone who is in the same position as me that will understand.

The big day arrived, Monday April the 10th 1972, and the place we were going to was Alwyn House at Ceres outside Cupar in Fife. We caught the nine o'clock train from Newcastle Central Station to Edinburgh then boarded another train to Cupar and a bus to Ceres. I already had butterflies in my stomach. My mam was my

CHAPTER 9

escort and together we arrived at Alwyn House at Ceres at twenty past one. Dinner was being served – it smelt delicious! I was starving and looking forward to it. We were greeted at the door by Mrs Fairley. She and her husband lived there, managed and ran the centre.

Our cases were taken from us and Mrs Fairley escorted us down the corridor to the dining room. It was a very long corridor with wood flooring and every step taken seemed to echo everywhere. As we entered the dining room I could hear many people talking; everyone else had already arrived and were busy eating their lunch – trust us to be the last two to arrive... we did get a little lost on the way though.

All the tables were full except one and there were two places left. Mrs Fairley took us over and introduced us to them. Raymond was twenty and one of the new trainees and was also registered blind and George his friend, who was much older, was his escort. Before we even entered the room my mam had looked through the window of the door and whispered to me quietly, "There he is just sitting over there waiting for you. I can only see his profile. He's dark, handsome and wearing a burgundy shirt."

At the time she didn't know if he was the new trainee or not but it turned out he was. I was put to sit beside him, Raymond was on my left, George on the right and my mam in front of me. They were both very pleasant and Raymond began to chat to me. I hadn't a clue what he was saying because he had such a broad Scottish accent. I just laughed and pretended that I understood. Raymond and George left the table before us and my mam couldn't believe how Raymond just stood up, picked his jacket off the back of the chair, flung it over his shoulder, turned and walked towards the door without any help.

I was so excited that I had been sitting beside him. I still had butterflies in my stomach. My mam told me how good looking he was. She was as excited as me and I couldn't wait to speak to him

again. After lunch Mrs Fairley took me upstairs to my bedroom. The girls were up and the boys were down. It was a huge place and a very tall building. The staircase was very wide and twisty and there were quite a few stairs to climb before you reached the first floor – that's where I was. I shared a bedroom with two other girls, Pamela and Helen. Mrs Fairley then showed me round the room. It was quite large; my bed was straight ahead and next to the window. We all had our own wardrobes but Pamela and I shared a dressing table.

Mrs Fairley began to tell me about the rules and regulations, the dos and don'ts. There was that many that if a secretary was here typing them up she would've needed a heck of a lot of paper. I wished I had a tape recorder I thought to myself but I would've probably run out of tape. It was ridiculous.

Mrs Fairley then took me back downstairs into the lounge where my mam was waiting. She was busy talking to Raymond but as soon as I entered the room and he heard my voice he rushed over to speak to me. He tripped over the large rug that was lying on the floor, stumbled and landed on his knees in front of me. We both laughed and carried on talking as if nothing had happened. Shortly afterwards, when Mrs Fairley had finished speaking to here, my mam started getting ready to go back home. Immediately Raymond spoke out and asked my mam if he could take me out for a drink that night. I was speechless and felt so embarrassed that my mam never hesitated and said yes straight away.

Raymond then turned and said, "Is that alright with you Mrs Fairley?"

She also agreed and seemed quite happy about it at the time. It was just as well I really liked him or I'd have been right up the creek. Everyone else had made their mind up for me! My stomach was churning over and over and my heart was beating fifty to the dozen and I was shaking with excitement. I wanted to say yes but at the same time I was very shy and withdrawn about going out on a date with a boy. This was much different from being with the lads and playing football and cricket – they were my mates.

All I came out with was "I don't drink" then my mam said "she likes a drink of coca cola".

Well that was it: I was going out on my first date with Raymond. I was hoping it was a date and not a casual get together or a one off. My mam and George left to go back home.

Shortly afterwards Raymond and I were taken upstairs to see Mr Fairley who was almost blind. He took us into the assembly room to work together and to test our coordination abilities. It was an average sized room and it was that hot it was difficult to breathe. Then Mr Fairley began to show us wooden shelves; they were very long and at different levels and they were made to look like boxes. Some were larger than others and there were dozens of them filled with different sized nuts, bolts, screws and strips of flat metal with holes going down the middle. It was like being in a DIY shop or a garage. Everything felt the same as my brothers' meccano set back home. I wanted to burst out laughing. I was wondering what on earth they wanted me to do with these. I don't think Mr Fairley would have been amused as he was a real miserable so and so.

We were both given the same objects that had already been made. Mr Fairley asked us both to copy them and said that he would be back in a couple of hours to see how we had got on. As soon as he left the room we both burst out into fits of laughter; we thought it was hilarious. There were four different shapes that we had to copy – a star, a hexagon… and I don't remember what the other two were.

Raymond and I were having a whale of a time. I couldn't believe how much I felt at ease with him considering we had just met. It seemed like we'd known each other for years and we got on like a house on fire. I had heard people talk about love at first sight and now I knew what they meant. I fell head over heels in love with Raymond the minute we met.

We waited well over two and a half hours for Mr Fairley to come back but we were sure he had forgotten all about us so we decided to try and find our own way back. However, we couldn't remember which way we'd came. We didn't realise there were different routes and we both nearly broke our necks almost falling down a narrow spiral staircase. We were holding onto each other trying to find our feet as we slipped on the stairs and bumped into the wall. Eventually we managed to get down in one piece and made our way to the lounge.

Just as we were about to go out that night Mrs Fairley advised us to go to the Meldrums Hotel as it was just a few minutes' walk down the road. Because it was our first day at Alwyn House she didn't want us to lose our way. We left at seven o'clock that evening and Mrs Fairley reminded us to be back by 10:30 because if we weren't the doors would be locked. She warned us not to be late!

The Meldrums was a small country hotel with a lounge where guests could eat. It had a small bar and a few bedrooms upstairs where guests would stay. Mrs Seith owned the hotel and ran it with the help of her family. She was a lovely little old lady, very pleasant and was always laughing.

Raymond and I sat in the bar where it was nice and cosy and had a lovely atmosphere. Mrs Seith sat us at a table in two beautiful wicker chairs which were facing each other and served us our drinks. Her daughter put on a record of Simon and Garfunkel singing Bridge over troubled water. Everything felt so magical and romantic. I was literally dying to go to the toilet but was terrified because I had a feeling that he would move his chair next to mine if I did, but unfortunately I couldn't hold on any longer and just had to go.

Sure enough when I came back his chair was next to mine. I began to feel anxious and was breaking out in a cold sweat. Poor Raymond – he only went to put his arm around my shoulders and hold my hand. I got such a fright that I pulled my shoulders away and said loudly, "What on earth are you doing?"

He quickly moved his hands away saying, "Sorry, I thought it would just be nice to put my arm around you and hold your hand."

Goodness knows what others thought that night. Raymond must've felt so embarrassed but he just carried on talking as if nothing had happened, probably to cover his embarrassment. After all that we still had a lovely evening. Although Alwyn House wasn't far away we left at 9.45 to make sure we were back in plenty of time. It was a beautiful night and we chatted while we walked up the road.

There was a bus stop just before the turning towards Alwyn House where Raymond stopped to give me a goodnight kiss. I was surprised he even tried after the way I'd behaved in the pub. I got such a shock that I quickly pushed him so hard he went flying backwards off the pavement and ended up on the ground in the middle of the road. He must have thought I was totally bonkers and the strangest person he had ever been out with. Just as well it was quiet and there were no cars about. I felt so terrible and embarrassed about what I had done. I apologized and said, "I don't like the idea of being kissed and please don't do it again as it frightens me."

Raymond then began to apologize. He was lovely and very understanding about it. Just as well.

I was absolutely furious with myself. *That's it, Christine, you've blown it big style*, I thought *there's no way he's going to ask you out again after this.*

We arrived back at Alwyn House about 10:00 that evening and guess who was there waiting to greet us – both Mr and Mrs Fairley. They were like the Gestapo the way they spoke to us. "You, my girl, get up those stairs now and I'll be up in a minute to see you," said Mrs Fairley and Mr Fairley went with Raymond to his room. I was shaking like a leaf and was wondering what I'd done wrong. I was thinking we were back in plenty of time so it can't be that. I was racking my brains and in she walked. She went berserk, ranting and raving like a possessed woman. She spoke so quickly and because of her broad Scottish accent I couldn't understand anything she was saying. I was that upset I began to cry and got told off for that as well.

I was now beginning to get the gist of the story and I was totally gutted and upset about the accusations she was making. She accused me of staying out all night with a complete stranger. She said I was no good and practically called me a slut and a tart and I was just like all the others who had been there before me. I was absolutely livid. I have always been brought up to respect my elders but she was off her head and way out of line and no matter how frightened I was of her there was no way I was going to sit back and let anyone make such terrible accusations like that about me. I plucked up the courage to say something but it didn't make any difference – she just bawled at me as her mind was already made up and nothing would change it. She was nothing but a stuck up hot headed Scottish cow. All I could think of was if this is what it's like after my first day here goodness knows what lies ahead.

There were people of all ages at Alwyn House and apparently Raymond and I were the only two newcomers that day which we didn't realise at the time. Some trainees had arrived the previous week and there were still more to come. There was a great bunch of people when we were there and we had many laughs amongst ourselves. The only downfall was that it was run by the Fairleys, two old goats who had no personality or sense of humour. Even the SS didn't have a look in, and from that night on they had it in for Raymond and me.

The following morning as we all walked down the corridor for breakfast Raymond and I briefly spoke about what had happened the night before. As we entered the dining room Raymond and I weren't too sure where to sit because everyone else must have had a set place as they all knew where to go. So we decided to go and sit at the same table where we first met but Mrs Fairley soon put a stop to that. We had just sat down when Mrs Fairley grabbed me by the scruff of the neck and dragged me over to sit with some others at a different table. I was stunned and felt so embarrassed.

Immediately after breakfast when we went to leave the room Mr and Mrs Fairley came over to me and Raymond and ordered us back to our rooms for another dressing down. They wanted to know what we had been talking about when we were walking down the corridor for breakfast. I told her that I'd said that I was hungry and looking forward to my breakfast. From that day on Raymond and I were not allowed to walk down the corridor together or even to sit at the same table for any meals. How ridiculous I thought, they treated us more like naughty school children rather than adults.

There were lots of different work rooms in the building where we went each day to learn new skills. For example braille, woodwork, typing, basket and cane work, how to use raffia cord to make different designs for stools and dining chairs and also how to use the old telephonist switchboard. The only doors in the building that didn't have glass in were the toilets and the bedrooms but I'm sure if the Fairleys had their own way there would have been glass in them to spy on us. Some of the trainees who had a little sight advised those of us who had none to be very careful about everything that we said and done because "the cooks, maids and the Fairleys spy on everyone here, they know every move you make".

One evening two of the trainees who had little sight came into the lounge and caught a glimpse of two maids sitting in the background. They had been watching and listening to all our conversations so that they could take everything back to the Fairleys. I often wondered how they knew so much. How sick is that! It made my flesh crawl. I didn't know people could stoop so low to do something like that.

No one was allowed to use a white cane in the buildings at all. Every person in the building had to knock at least two or three times on each door before opening it so that all of us trainees would be aware that someone was standing on the other side, which made a lot of sense and would help to avoid many accidents. We were shown once round the building and at the same time taken to many different rooms that we would be working in, then after that you were on your own. At first it was sometimes easy to lose your bearings and get lost in the building especially if you were the last one to leave class and got separated from others. It was up to you to remember where you were and find your way about. You soon got sick of walking into walls and doors and in the wrong places but it certainly made you get your act together. There was no mollycoddling or someone to take you round by the hand or wipe your nose and backside whilst you were there; you just had to get on with it.

Rain, hail or snow, every morning after breakfast we had to go on a two to three mile walk in the country and back. I think most of us felt it was the best part of the day. Fresh air, freedom, and two hours away from the Fairleys, yippee! And of course the best part for me was that I would be able to spend some time with Raymond. We would all hurry down to the bottom of the corridor, grab our coats off the pegs and each pick a white walking stick up and off we would go. As we walked down to the bottom of the drive we all had to pair up. Raymond and I would hang back for each other at the end of the queue so we could walk together. After we had walked about two hundred yards down the road and thought we were out of sight from Alwyn House sometimes Raymond and I would stop, turn and stick our fingers up in the air and shout 'up yours Fairley, you can't stop us now' and we would laugh about it. It was amazing how we were all adapting to our new way of life at Alwyn House. Everything was such a new adventure but an exciting one. It wasn't easy at first but I began to learn new skills which I thought I would never be able to do and most probably would never have done if it hadn't been for losing my sight.

My confidence was beginning to grow day by day and I was now able to do some of the simple things in life which I once used to do and always took for granted. We all enjoyed going on our walks but we certainly had to keep our wits about us as some of the time we were on main country roads as well as being in the valley and cutting through the countryside. Some of us would be singing, others talking and telling jokes but the staff always reminded us that the walks weren't entirely for the pleasure of it but also to learn to absorb the unknown surroundings.

Mr McKenzie and Miss Allen were both registered blind and had lost most of their sight many years ago. They were much older than most of us so obviously they had many years of experience and plenty of time to adapt to their loss of sight over the years. But there was no exception made at all for us new trainees. We were all in the same boat and always seemed to be chucked in the deep end with everything we were taught. You could either sink and go under or swim and rise above everything and get on with it; we were all survivors. We were taught how to walk safely in the country so that we could manage and be as normal as any other sighted person and fellwalker out there.

Sometimes we had to stride out at one heck of a pace just to keep up with each other. No wonder, when John Dark was in the front with the group leaders. He was sixty years old, six foot six inches tall and built like a tank. John was also totally blind. He had been a sergeant major in the army for many years and I'm sure on these walks he still thought he was marching on parade. He was a great guy who had bags of confidence and feared nothing. I think that a little of John Dark rubbed off on most of us – well I know he did with me. I bet when sighted walkers passed us on the way they would never have realised or believed that none of us could see as we all managed so well. The only give-away would have been our white walking sticks but then again it's amazing how many sighted people don't pay attention or take notice of many things. They probably wouldn't have even noticed.

I'll never forget the day when Raymond and I got separated from the others on the walk. We were too busy talking to each other when suddenly we realised just how quiet it was. We began to shout for the others but there was no response. We hadn't a clue where we were or how far we had dropped behind as we hadn't been paying any attention. Because we were young and daft we thought it was hilarious and a big joke. Our reaction at first was they'll soon realise we are missing and send someone out to look for us.

A few minutes later it dawned on us that nobody would be coming back to find us at all because we remembered that it had been explained to us very clearly from the very beginning how important it was to pay attention to everything that was taught to us when outside, especially being in the country. At any time if any of you get lost, remember that you are on your own and you will have to use all the skills you have been taught to find your own way back.

At the time I thought it was cruel but being realistic that's what real life is all about. Yes it can be cruel, tough, heart rending, painful and sometimes seem unfair but if our life was like a bed of roses and everything was handed to us on a silver platter and always 'hunky dory' what would be the point in living? We would have learned nothing, have no skills, no understanding, feelings or compassion, so how could we begin to help anyone or give some advice? There would be no goals to set or achievements to reach and fulfill, nothing to strive for or look forward to. There would be no excitement in our lives, so again what would be the point of living? How we live our lives is up to us and also what we do with it. We all make mistakes and I have made many but we must try to learn from them. I have been knocked down time and time again and my confidence shattered and destroyed over and over, but because of this it has helped to make me a stronger person and more determined than ever to do something with my life.

Ceres was a very small village with one long main street, the

Meldrum on the right and a church on the left. Further up the road was the fish shop and on the opposite side a small chemist and a small store with the post office inside. Round the corner there was a small pub called the Ceres Inn and opposite was another pub with a small museum attached to it. I suppose anyone driving through who wasn't familiar with the area could've missed it all.

On a Saturday night most of us went to the Ceres Inn which was run by Jim White and his wife. It was a tiny little pub with a larger room downstairs where there was music. The atmosphere was electric; everyone was so friendly and made us feel welcome. They had a small amplifier with a mike where people would sing and dance Scottish songs all night. There was even a piper and when he played the room vibrated with the sound. They all certainly knew how to enjoy themselves and have a good time. I had never enjoyed myself as much anywhere as I did in that little pub all those years ago with those wonderful people. I will cherish those memories forever.

Afterwards we'd all call in the fish shop and get a bag of chips and take a slow walk back to Alwyn House. We'd all be in fits of laughter; you couldn't help it when Roy and Pamela were about – they were both a scream and had a wicked sense of humour. If any of our spirits were down they would most certainly pick them up. We all gelled so well together and became good friends and enjoyed so much of that moment in time.

On alternative Saturdays we were allowed to go to Cupar for the day which was a few miles away and was the local town for shopping. It was quite a large town with many good shops, cafes, pubs and restaurants there. We had been taken in by the staff through the week so that we could get familiar with the area in finding our way about. We were all given a white telescopic (folding) cane to use and taught how to use it correctly which was much different from our white wooden walking sticks.

The Saturdays we went into Cupar I think most of us finished our breakfast in record time because we didn't want to be late and miss the bus as they ran very few and far between going and coming back. We would dash out of Alwyn House as if there was no tomorrow and when the bus arrived most of us would rush on like a bunch of excited school children who were going on an outing for the day. We all had a fantastic time and made the most of every minute.

Also on alternative weekends we were allowed to go home. Most of the trainees came from different parts of Scotland. Unfortunately there were others who came from other parts of the country which was too far to travel for a weekend. So those trainees who lived relatively local would offer to take another trainee home with them, but some trainees had no option at all and had to stay at Alwyn House.

Raymond lived in Edinburgh and had invited me to go home to meet his family for the first time. He came from a place called Leith which was near the docks. Although I was looking forward to meeting them I couldn't help but feel a little anxious. Raymond was the youngest of six. He was dying to show me off and kept telling me not to worry – "they'll all love you like I do".

I couldn't help but think how all their eyes would be fixed on me and because I was a plain Jane I thought they might all be disappointed and felt he could have done better. My mind was racing away and I hoped and prayed that they would approve of and like me. I had never been to Edinburgh before. The furthest I'd ever been away was when my mam and Aunt Florrie took us to our local seaside resort at Tynemouth in King Edward's Bay when I was young which was roughly ten miles away from where we lived. So going to Edinburgh was a new and exciting adventure for me which I was really enjoying.

As soon as I met Raymond's family all my anxieties disappeared; I have never felt so welcomed – they were they salt of the earth. I felt so happy and pleased to be there. I had never felt as good as this in

CHAPTER 9

years – not since I lived at Back Villa Place where I was born.

Time was flying by – I couldn't believe I'd been at Alwyn House just over six weeks now, seven more to go. Raymond will be twenty-one shortly on 20th June. We got on like a house on fire and were very much in love. I felt that my life was just beginning; I was so in love and excitedly looking forward to the future. I hoped and prayed that Raymond would always be part of it. I sometimes wondered just what it was that Raymond saw in me and how we were still together when I hadn't even let him kiss me yet. I knew it was just a simple little thing to do but I found it so difficult. How ridiculous and stupid was that. Raymond kept telling me not to worry about it and he was quite prepared to wait as long as it took. I really hoped he meant it! I couldn't bear the thought that Raymond might forget all about me and not keep in touch after we leave Alwyn House. My life would not be the same.

A few days later, during the week, one evening Raymond, Roy and I went out for a quiet drink to the Ceres Inn. It was ten o'clock and we were just about to leave when Roy broke down crying; he was in a terrible state. Roy would be about twenty five and was feeling quite depressed and wanted to talk to us in confidence about what was bothering him. He asked us to promise not to tell anyone, especially not the Fairleys, about what happened that night, and we honoured that.

We knew we were going to be late back and in deep trouble that evening because the doors shut at 10.30pm. But Roy needed us that night no matter what the consequences were. There was no way we were going to turn our back on him. We arrived back at Alwyn House ten minutes late that night and sure enough the doors were locked. As we knocked on the door the three of us were wondering what was going to happen. Mr Fairley opened it and asked who was there. He pretended to be shocked and thought we were in bed. We knew he was lying. He ordered us immediately to go into the lounge. My stomach was churning over and over, I was trembling inside. Mr Fairley was furious. We tried to apologise and said to him we'd lost track of time but he wasn't having any of it. His attitude was ridiculous. You would have thought we had committed a serious crime. I was terrified of him!

Roy and I said very little that night; even if we had spoken he would have shouted us down, humiliated us and torn us to shreds. He was a dictator, he wouldn't listen to what we had to say; we couldn't reason with him and what he said went. However Mr Fairley couldn't get the better of Raymond because he gave as good as he got. Raymond was strong willed and wasn't frightened of him at all and always stood up for what he thought was right but was never cheeky to him – but Mr Fairley didn't like that and it made him more angry. He just went on and on and the things he said were terrible. He was way out of line that night and there was no need for it.

Roy and I were dismissed from the room and ordered to bed but Raymond was told to stay exactly where he was as he hadn't finished with him yet. He really had it in for Raymond. I was in a terrible state that night and hardly slept. The following morning after breakfast I managed to catch up with Raymond in the lounge. I was devastated when Raymond told me he was going back home within the next hour.

Apparently Mr Fairley had told him to pack his bags and leave. I was totally gutted and everyone was appalled about what the Fairleys had done. It should never have been allowed but no one else had a say in the matter bar them. After Raymond left I felt really down. I was missing him terribly but he kept his promise and phoned me every night from a neighbour's house. It wasn't the same at Alwyn House without Raymond being there but I just had to carry on and make the most of it. He had only been gone a week when I took poorly at Alwyn House. Apparently I had taken a really bad fit. It sounded like the same type I used to have some time ago when I was in hospital. I hadn't taken a fit like that in ages as the

My parents Jean and John Pattinson on their wedding day

Me on the right with my twin brother John

Me aged 5

Nana Gardner

Me, John and Jackie

Me aged 11

Me aged 13

Me with Dad Hall

Me with parasol

The wedding line-up

On our wedding day - 19 June 1976

new medication I was on was managing to control them.

Epilepsy was a very complicated illness in those days and still is today. Most people associate fits with dropping to the floor, shaking and going into a state of unconsciousness. They are what you call grand mals. But there are many other different types of fits – some people can actually be awake during them, walk about, shout, be very angry and act with a very bizarre behaviour. Those were the type I took as well as the grand mals. After they were over apparently I would carry on as if nothing had ever happened and remember nothing about it.

But many years ago because of doctors and man's ignorance many epileptic sufferers were incorrectly diagnosed and were classed and treated like mental freaks. Some were put into asylums and others into mental institutions for the rest of their lives. I am so grateful that I was one of the lucky ones to have got out because of the female doctor that was there at that particular time. Looking back I strongly believe that she was a guardian angel sent just for me.

But what about the hundreds if not thousands of other innocent people who have been locked up and put away into horrible, dreadful places like that through no fault of their own just because society and do-gooders have decided to wash their hands of them? Even young girls who had children out of wedlock were also put into these dreadful places and forgotten about. Even today there will be many of those people still alive and locked away. Personally I still find it so hard to comprehend and understand how those who were held responsible for making such drastic and malicious decisions in those days were allowed to get away with it. They have deprived, wiped out and destroyed many young innocent people's lives forever.

I have just woken up and I am lying in bed; two ambulance men have just introduced themselves to me. They said they had been called out to Alwyn House because I had taken a fit in the lounge downstairs. I can't remember anything about it.

They asked how I was feeling. I hardly got the words out of my mouth when Mr Fairley rudely interrupted in a very abrupt manner demanding the ambulance men to remove me immediately out of the building. He made me feel like a piece of old furniture that needed to be removed and chucked out on to the tip the way he said it. I felt so upset that I began to cry.

One of the ambulance men sat down on the bed beside me and held my hand whilst the other man went over to the bedroom door where Mr Fairley was standing to give him a piece of his mind. The ambulance man next to me asked if would I like a cup of tea and did I smoke. I said yes to both, "but you're not allowed to smoke in the bedrooms here," I explained.

He then replied, "Well, Christine, today we are going to break all the rules," and laughed.

Mr Fairley was still giving the other ambulance man what for – he hadn't heard what was said until we actually lit up. He soon smelt the smoke and was furious and went into another frenzy, shouting at us to put the cigarettes out as it was totally forbidden for anyone to smoke in the bedrooms here. Again Mr Fairley demanded that he wanted me to be removed immediately from the premises "and I mean now. I want you to take her to that hospital down the road, you know the one I mean!"

I nearly died when the ambulance driver jumped off the bed and charged across the room towards him; he had just pushed his luck a little too far this time. "As I said earlier, Mr Fairley, we are breaking all the rules here today and let's just get one thing straight here: you might be in charge of this bloody place but you're not in charge of me and don't you stand there making threats and demands. I will take Christine from here when I feel she's ready to go. As far as I'm concerned there's no need or reason to take her anywhere. I can't understand why you won't let her stay and finish her course. She's only had a fit for God's sake."

But Mr Fairley had already made his mind up. "I've already phoned and told her mother to come and pick her up."

The ambulance driver said, "Why don't you let her wait until she arrives?"

"No way," he replied, "because there's no trains through to Cupar until tomorrow and I want her out of here as soon as possible."

When I was eventually ready and packed to leave the ambulance men escorted me downstairs and guess who was waiting for us at the bottom? Mr Fairley. He remarked again to the ambulance men. "I hope you are taking her to that hospital down the road there, that's where she needs to be. You know which one I mean," he kept saying.

One of the ambulance drivers said to him in a very stern voice, "I won't tell you again, Mr Fairley, you don't tell me what to do. Christine is my patient and I will take her where I feel she needs to go, not where you think she should be. I've heard a lot about you and this damn place and how it's run and believe you me it hasn't all been good. I always like to keep an open mind about everything but after what's happened here today my eyes have certainly been opened and don't think you've heard the last from me yet because you haven't. I'll be putting a full report in about you so be well prepared."

I was so surprised when Mr Fairley just stood there, said nothing and took it all. Maybe he realised that he'd over stepped his mark this time and thought it was better to keep his tongue between his teeth, I don't know.

The drivers told me they would only be a few minutes and to make my way to the front of the building and wait for them as they had to go and see to some business concerning the ambulance – I can't remember exactly what it was. I was just about to walk through the passageway to the front door when Mr Fairley stopped me in my tracks by placing his hand on my shoulder and spoke in a very nasty manner. He said: "I want to know the names of all the hospitals you've been into because as long as I'm alive I'm going to make sure you never ever get a job anywhere and I mean that, so you better be prepared, my girl."

By this time I was feeling totally fed up about everything; I'd had a bellyful of the Fairleys and Alwyn House and just wanted to get away as quickly as I could and as far away as possible. I noticed how he didn't have the bottle to pull me up in front of the ambulance men again – he was probably too frightened in case they chewed him up and spat him out. As far as I was concerned he was a right frigging coward, a bastard and a little squirm. I was pleased I was leaving and getting well rid of him.

The ambulance men came back to pick me up, escorted me into the ambulance and off we went. Although the ambulance men were great with me I couldn't help but feel a little anxious and wonder where I was being taken to. They had told me the name but it meant nothing to me. I was dying to ask them about the hospital that Mr Fairley had kept on talking about; I was waiting patiently, hoping that the drivers would tell me, but maybe they thought I had suffered enough grief for one day without them adding to it. I can't remember how far we had travelled but it seemed as if I had been in the ambulance for ages. All of a sudden the driver shouted, "It won't be long now, Christine, we're almost there."

I couldn't wait any longer as I desperately wanted to know, so I asked them again, "What type of hospital was it that Mr Fairley wanted you to take me to?"

"Don't worry about that, love, that's not going to happen," he said.

"I know that, but I still really need to know."

"Well, let's put it this way, sweetheart," he said. "If we had taken you to that hospital I can definitely guarantee that you would never have got out of it."

I wasn't that shocked when he told me because deep down

I already knew. I just needed to hear it. Can you imagine if the ambulance men had been on the same wavelengths as Mr Fairley and had agreed with him? I would never have been here today to tell the story.

Chapter 10

We've just arrived at the hospital; I'm pleased I'm only here for one night. My mam will be arriving tomorrow afternoon to take me back home. I hope she will be in a good frame of mind when she arrives because I couldn't take any more hassle. It's just dawned on me that Raymond will be phoning Alwyn House tonight. The kiosk is near the lounge; I hope someone will pick it up and explain what has happened. I could kick myself for not asking Raymond his neighbour's telephone number simply because it was easier for him to call me. Although I have been to his home I don't even know his address, I can't even remember if I gave him mine or told him it over the phone as everything happened so quickly when he left last week and I can't imagine the Fairleys giving anything away. At the moment I just want to burst into tears. I feel as sick as a dog about everything.

The journey back home wasn't too bad. My Mam said very little and didn't show much concern as usual. I was pleased in some respects because the way I was feeling I didn't want to talk to anyone. My head was buzzing; it was so full and tired I couldn't switch off, but how I wished I could. It was racing over and over going fifty to the dozen thinking about everything that had happened in the last week. I couldn't believe how one minute my life was so full and rich and bursting with excitement, I was on cloud nine and so happy. Then the next minute it's all taken away from you and you're feeling back in the depths of despair. I felt as if someone had just picked up a great big hammer and was continuously knocking me on the head like a tent peg pushing me further and further into the ground. It's awful, I hate feeling like this; it seems as if it's out of my control and I can't do anything about it.

We've just arrived home. I briefly said hello to everyone then went straight up to my room. I'm pleased to be in here as I feel safe now because I know no one will come in to disturb me.

The following week was dreadful. I spent most of my time in bed. I could hardly eat and didn't want to talk to anyone. I couldn't stop thinking about Raymond and the fun we'd shared together. I kept waiting for a letter to arrive and hoped he would either find or get my address one way or another. I was trying so hard to keep my spirits high but when you're feeling depressed and rock bottom it's always easier said than done.

No one had a clue how I was feeling or even took the time to find out. I was feeling so angry about everything, everyone, especially the big man upstairs, God. I don't know how many times I had my boxing gloves on with him, I was always lashing out and giving him a piece of my mind and he always got the blame for everything.

The day I had been waiting for had eventually arrived. I was still lying in bed with the blankets over my head when my mam knocked at the door to come in and tell me that a letter had arrived from Edinburgh. "It must be from Raymond," she said in a very low key voice and then left the room.

Immediately I threw the blankets back and leapt out of bed. I was so overjoyed and began to jump up and down in the air shouting yes, yes, yes with excitement. Just as well my bedroom was above the washhouse so no one could hear me. I grabbed my dressing gown and rushed downstairs as quickly as I could. My heart was pounding so fast and beating with excitement that I thought it was going to burst open. I sat down on the settee and waited patiently for my mam to begin. It was so good to hear from Raymond. This was the best news I could have ever received; I needed it so much and it picked me up no end.

After my mam had finished reading the letter she put it back into the envelope and handed it to me. I went straight back upstairs to my bedroom, jumped on to the bed, still clutching the letter in my hand. I was so happy and couldn't stop smiling and I felt as if my face was beaming. I was trying to remember everything Raymond had said in the letter and was going over and over everything in my mind. I didn't want to forget anything.

I found it very hard and distressing knowing that someone else had to read and write my personal letters for me. I would be so frustrated; it made me feel so useless and helpless it was like a big slap in the face always reminding you about your disability. I just couldn't stand it and often went on a downer because of it.

Raymond and I missed each other terribly; we couldn't wait to see one another again. Every other month I would travel up to Edinburgh and stay with Raymond's family for at least two to three weeks or sometimes even a month, and on an odd occasion my mam would invite Raymond to come and stay with us for a week or two.

In between writing letters we would try to make arrangements to phone one another on a certain night. Very few people had phones in those days. Raymond would phone from his friend's house. I used to have to go to the telephone kiosk at the top of our street, and for a while my younger brother Laurie or my younger sister Kerry would take me up. But my mam soon put a stop to that. She was quite a loud person and swore like a trooper, it was just like God Bless You and part of her everyday language. She was never crude and some of her sayings would be quite funny and you couldn't help but laugh. Her language was quite normal to all of us and we thought nothing about it.

"So! Raymond's phoning you tonight," my mam said. "Well, I hope you realise that no one's taking you to the telephone kiosk tonight. As a matter of fact no bugger's gonna take you anywhere again or even do anything for you anymore. Do you hear that, everyone?" she shouted loudly.

There was this deadly silence and I just stood there in shock!

"You know where the frigging telephone box is," she said. "It's still in the same place as it was last week and the week before that – it hasn't went anywhere. You complained about the Fairleys being as hard as nails – they might've been, but by God it did the bloody trick, didn't it? It made you do things for yourself because you had to whether you liked it or not. What was the friggin point of you going to Alwyn House?" she shouted loudly! "What was the bloody point of it all? You've come back here and allowed yourself to be as useless and as helpless as you were before you sodding well went away. Is that what you want, Christine, for the rest of your life? Someone to take you by the hand, lead you everywhere, do everything for you, even wipe your frigging arse for you all the time? Is that what you really want, Christine?" she shouted. "Is that what you frigging well want for the rest of your life?"

I couldn't find the words to say anything and just stood there quietly. Nobody said a word. My body felt numb from top to bottom. I had a big lump in the back of my throat, my lips were beginning to quiver, my eyes were filling up. I fought back the tears and was determined not to cry.

"As from now there's certainly going to be some bloody changes in this house," my mam said. "I'm gonna be twice as hard as the Fairleys. I want you to stand on your own two feet, do you hear me, on your own two frigging feet! I want you to be able to look after yourself and not to depend on anyone. There's no reason why you can't do the same things as any bugger else. You did it before, didn't you? For God's sake, you've only lost your bloody eyesight and nothing else – what the hell's the matter with you?"

My mam then charged from the living room into the kitchen. I wasn't too sure what she was going to do so I just stood there like a wet blanket quivering inside. She was back in seconds and grabbed one of my hands and hung a bucket on it and placed my other one round the nozzle of the Hoover.

CHAPTER 10

"There's plenty of work to be done in this house; you used to do it all at one time. I think you've had a long enough break, don't you? Well now it's back to the grindstone. The bedrooms, toilet, bathroom and stairs need doing. You've got everything there that you need to do it with so get on with it," she said. "Don't stand there like that or otherwise nothing's going to get done. You'll manage; you don't need eyes to clean up with, just a pair of hands. You've got a brain – use it."

I was so upset and could feel the lump in my throat getting bigger and bigger. I knew my mam meant every word she said and there was no going back on it. I picked the Hoover up and slowly carried it up the stairs, then I came back down and filled my bucket with water. I was just about to start and my mam shouted up, "Don't forget to check all the floors, mind, make sure there's nothing lying about. I don't want you sucking anything up the Hoover and breaking it and watch where you're putting that bucket. Don't be knocking it over otherwise we'll be flooded out."

At the time she made me feel so worthless and cheap as if the Hoover and a little spillage were more important than I was. Eventually I got down on my hands and knees and began to grovel and feel around the floor. Because I had two brothers and a sister who were younger than I was I knew there would be toys and other things lying all over the place. I was more bothered about banging my head or hurting myself by kneeling on something. I felt just like a dog on all fours, scavenging around hoping to find something. I couldn't fight back the tears any longer. I began to cry. I was so upset, frustrated and pissed off about everything.

Later that afternoon after I had finished doing all my chores, there was no thanks, word of encouragement... nothing! All my mam could say was, "Raymond's phoning you tonight, isn't he?"

"Yes," I replied.

"Well, don't forget, like I said earlier, you're on your own tonight going up to that phone box. It's up to you whether you go up or not,

I'm not bothered. It depends how important you feel your phone call is. Also, whilst we're on the subject, if you want anything from the shops in the future again, you know where they are."

"That's fine by me," I said. "I'll manage."

I was trying to put a brave face on and pretend that it didn't bother me, but deep down I was totally crapping myself. It's not that the telephone kiosk or the shops were too far away or too difficult to get to. It was just the thought of having to go out into the big wide world on my own for the first time, not being able to see. What made me feel more nervous than ever was knowing that my family and probably half of the street would all be watching out of their windows to see if I'd got lost or made any mistakes. I couldn't bear the thought of it. But there was no way out and I knew I had to do it. I went upstairs and sat down on my bed and began to give myself a good talking to. *Come on Christine,* I said, *for goodness sake get a grip of yourself, it's no big deal, you can do it, you know you can.*

I know it might sound stupid but by doing this it helped to boost my morale and confidence. I also thought about everything I had learned. I began to visualise the street and draw a picture of it in my head to see what was the best, safest and easiest way to get to where I was going and back again. It was so important to me to get it right without making any mistakes. I wanted to prove to my mam more than anyone but also to myself that I could do it on my own without any help.

Because of what my mam said and made me do on that day I thought she was heartless, cruel and that she didn't love or care about me at all, but looking back over the years I've realised It's true that sometimes you have to be cruel to be kind, as the old saying goes.

That particular day my mam certainly made me stand on my own two feet. I felt it was a big challenge and the amount of confidence I gained from that day was second to none. For the first time I began to believe in myself; it gave me so much courage that I now felt more confident and wanted to move on and try to do other things. If it had not been for my mam being so forceful, abrupt and quite cruel sometimes I would certainly not be the strong successful woman that I am today. I have so much to thank her for. But it still does not excuse her from the many other things that she said and done.

A few days later I received a visit from Mr Gray, my B.P.R.O. at social services. I could tell by his voice that it wasn't good news. "I have just received a letter from Mr Fairley at Alwyn House," he said. I knew what he was going to say as soon as he opened his mouth.

Unfortunately it *was* bad news. *I knew it, the bastard* I thought to myself.

"I can't discuss all the contents of the letter with you," he said, "but what I can tell you is that Mr Fairley has certainly made sure that we can't consider or even allow you to seek employment anywhere. I'm sorry, Christine, but our hands are tied and there's nothing we can do about it. Mr Fairley carries a lot of clout."

What a bastard, I thought to myself again, *he was nothing but a frigging piece of shit*. Again please pardon my French but that was exactly my thought, a great big fucking piece of rotten shit. There was this long pause. I think my mam and Mr Gray were waiting for my response. I was determined to stay calm, cool and collected. I didn't want anyone to know my thoughts or how I was feeling – this was between me and the four walls of my bedroom where I could let off steam in private and again no one would ever know.

"Well Mr Gray, what happens next?" I asked.

"Well there's this fantastic new place which has been purposely built and designed for the disabled called fountain view. It's just down the road from here near the Bensham Hospital where the disabled can go for occupational therapy. I think you'll like it there," he replied.

There's that word again, I thought, *disabled*. At the time it made me feel like a freak as if I was branded with the name across my

forehead for everyone to see. I agreed to give it a try and thought
anything's going to be better than sitting around here all day. The
bus picked me up each day around ten o'clock in the morning and
returned after three thirty in the afternoon.

It was the most amazing place. The building was huge and it
even had its own private club attached to it where non-disabled
people could also come along and join as members. It had a massive
concert room with a lounge, snooker room, TV room and even a
quiet room where you could go and sit and listen to records. The
work side comprised of two large craft rooms, a woodwork and
metalwork room and even a place to make pottery. There were
people of all ages and different disabilities, some more severe than
others and there were even those who were mentally handicapped. I
was one of the youngest and it was like one big happy family. We all
got on well together, helped one another, looked after each other
and the staff were terrific. Everyone was treated equal and like
normal human beings, they made you forget you had a disability
and that's the way it should be. The amount of different products
that were made and produced by the members were remarkable,
from blanket chests to wrought iron garden furniture, telephone
tables, dolls houses, sledges – you name it they did it.

There was one girl who had lost the use of her arms and
one leg and yet turned out the most amazing pictures and even
sketches on table mats and coasters all done by using her mouth.
Everything was made to the highest standard for the public and
small businesses to buy. I did stool seating with fabric for children's
rocking chairs and made all different items with cane. There was
nothing in this work place that these people couldn't do. They put
many able bodied people to shame including myself. Everyone
was so happy go lucky, even making jokes and fun about their own
disability but the main thing that struck me was that there was no
self-pity here or even anyone saying 'why me?'. They just all seemed
to get on with their lives, in what they were doing with no moans

and groans.

They put me to shame and I felt so humble before them that it helped me to remember how important it was to always keep my life and thoughts in order as it made me feel so grateful for everything that I had. I began to think how minor my disability was compared to theirs and eventually that word disability didn't haunt me anymore. It was just a name and identity for others to understand and being here with these people who became my friends gave me great encouragement and determination. My confidence was growing rapidly day by day and I was now more determined than ever to get out there and make my mark in life, but most of all to prove Mr Fairley wrong – that one day I will get a job.

I was just eighteen and there was no way that I was going to allow this control freak and arsehole to win and destroy my life forever. That same year when Raymond came down to stay with us we went out one evening with my mam and dad to the Sunniside Social Club. We had a great night as they used to have some very good turns on. When we all got back Raymond and I went into the sitting room. I was totally gobsmacked when Raymond all of sudden got down on one knee took my hand, proposed and asked me to marry him. I can still remember that day as if it were yesterday, it was magical. I was so happy and overjoyed and thought I was the most luckiest person in all the world and couldn't imagine spending my life with anyone else but Raymond.

We were so madly and deeply in love with each other. I would be nineteen on December 30th but we decided to get engaged on Christmas Day that year. For me Christmas had a far more special meaning to it. We held the engagement party at my mam and dad's house. Raymond's mam and his sister Gloria managed to come down and my parents invited a few of their friends from the club. It was such a magical evening, everyone was so happy for us and enjoying themselves; for Raymond and I that moment in time was the best day of our life. We hadn't yet made plans for our wedding day – it would probably be in a few years' time. My dream wedding had always been to be married in white with three or four bridesmaids and a couple of page boys. It would take a lot of money so we would have to save up hard.

Since Raymond left Alwyn House his B.P.R.O. has tried everywhere to seek employment for him but unfortunately with no success as jobs were very hard to come by in Edinburgh. Many firms in those days were very reluctant to employ disabled people – although they had to take a certain percentage, if they could get out of it they would. Before Raymond lost his eyesight he worked as a labourer for a small roofing company; he loved working outdoors and doing physical work. At break times he enjoyed sitting on the rooftops talking to his work mates. He would have a sandwich in one hand and drink tea from his treacle tin in the other while overlooking the views and watching life go by.

It's February 1973 and my mam has been acting very strange lately and I don't know why. My two younger brothers and sister have just come in from school. Everyone is settling down and watching TV.

All of a sudden there was a loud knock at the front door. I was sitting at the far end of the room and was wondering why no one else had bothered to get up and answer it. It was loud enough for us all to hear and quite obvious that nobody else was going to get up and move so I decided to get up and do it. I got the shock of my life when I opened the front door and heard Raymond's voice. He immediately dropped his cases down on the ground outside, rushed into the passageway, whisked me off my feet and swung me round with excitement. I was totally speechless.

Unbeknown to me, my mam had been making plans for Raymond to come down and live with us. It was now all beginning to make sense; I had wondered why she had decided to move us all into different bedrooms. I was now sharing with my younger siblings Kerry and Laurie, John and Raymond were to share next door, my younger brother Robert was in the front bedroom, and my Mam and Dad have taken my old bedroom over above the wash house.

My Mam said, "I thought if Raymond was living down here with us he'd stand a better chance in finding a job here so you'll be able to save up for when you get married."

At first I couldn't believe that my mam had gone to all this trouble for me, well for both of us really, to help give us a start in life. Well I hope that's why she's done it – at the minute I'm not too sure… only time will tell.

Raymond was very popular down here and everyone got on well with him especially my dad; they had a good relationship. "You've got a good one there, Christine," everyone would say, "keep tight hold of him."

Raymond's father was Italian; his name was Gaetano Deponio. He was born in a small village somewhere near Monte Cassino and lived with his family there until the age of seven. In 1912 his parents Benedetto Deponio and Rosa Sidonio Deponio decided to emigrate and bring the rest of their children to Scotland to live because war had broken out in Italy at the time. We don't know the exact village the family came from as they did not arrive with any birth certificates but what we do know is that it was near Monte Cassino.

Raymond's mother was Scottish; her name was Frances Fraser Martin Murdoch and she was born in a small village called Tranent in East Lothian in Scotland. Gaetano was the only one of his family who married outside of his culture and together they ran their own fish and chip shop in their home town Leith in Edinburgh where the whole family mucked in.

Unfortunately Raymond's dad died in 1969. My only regret is that I never had the pleasure of meeting him. Apparently he was a wonderful man, greatly loved by his family and well respected by everyone who knew him. People used to tell me how handsome and good looking Raymond was, probably because of his dark hair and tanned skin. He has obviously inherited the Italian genes.

He wasted no time in looking for a job when he came down to live with us. He made it quite clear that he wouldn't be waiting around for any B.P.R.O.'s help and was determined to find a job on his own. Raymond had lost most of his sight over a period of six weeks and was registered blind in 1972 and before he came to Alwyn House he had already received some mobility training.

When Raymond went along to the job centre in Gateshead he was adamant about going on his own because he was that independent. "I'll be fine, I won't get lost if that's what you think," he said.

He was totally fearless about doing anything or going anywhere. You only had to show him once how to get somewhere or do something. Even when he was taken around a building, village or a town for the first time he would remember every detail, nook and cranny as he was diagnosed with having almost a hundred per cent mobility and a photographic memory. He could almost out-do and leave any sighted person standing. He was truly a remarkable and amazing guy.

Raymond had only been gone a few hours when he returned to tell us that he was going for an interview at Kavli's cheese factory the following Monday. We all thought he was having us on but it was true. I was totally thrilled, gobsmacked and speechless all at the same time. Kavli was part of Primula, a factory that produced Primula cheese on the Team Valley Trading Estate just down the road from where we lived. It was one of the largest industrial estates in the country. There were hundreds of different factories, buildings, warehouses and shops there. Most of them were surrounded by trees, lawns and flowerbeds. Over the weekend my dad showed Raymond the best way how to get there and back from Kavli's safely for his interview on that Monday.

It's 9:00 Monday morning and Raymond has just left for his interview; we all had our fingers crossed and prayed that he would get the job.

He was so pleased and grateful that the company had taken the time to offer him an interview – that's all he ever wanted, just a chance to get his foot in the door to hopefully sell and prove himself. Apparently Kavli in those days had a very good track record in employing disabled people. Raymond was very confident and outgoing and if anyone could sell themselves it would be him. For a long time he would not accept that he had a disability or that he was even blind – as far as he was concerned there was nothing wrong with him and he was as normal as the next person. It was a very sore subject of which you always stayed away from and maybe that's why he managed everything so well.

We all waited patiently that day hoping it would be good news. My mam had just caught a glimpse of Raymond walking up the garden path – he had been away the best part of the day and my stomach had never stopped churning all morning. I couldn't bring myself to answer the front door so my dad went instead. My mam and I just stood there waiting; the tension was terrible.

Raymond slowly opened the sitting room door and quietly took a few paces forward. We were all anxious and never uttered a word. You could have heard a pin drop. Then all of a sudden he shouted, "I've got the job, Kirsty. I've got a job. I can't believe it!"

My mam and dad were just as pleased as we were. Raymond and I couldn't stop hugging each other with excitement. I was so happy for him, he really deserved it, so we both went out that evening to celebrate the good news. We felt on top of the world.

Raymond was to start his new job the following week and was on a month's trial. He was classed as a cheese scraper and his daily routine entailed picking up blocks of cheese weighing twenty pounds and over and then placing them on to a large lathe, then using a very sharp-bladed knife to remove the wax from them whilst it was spinning at a very high speed. The cheese was then put into a large mixing machine where it was all blended together to make different flavoured cheeses. He would certainly have to have his wits about him and to take care in what he was doing as it could be quite a dangerous job. He didn't just have to convince himself he could do it but also the management and staff.

"Nothing's a problem, I'll manage," he said to them. "It'll be a doddle, you'll see, I'll prove it to you all."

Everything was a doddle to Raymond – it was one of his favourite sayings and expressions.

Chapter 11

From the age of turning thirteen up until I lost my sight I used to do karate. It was brilliant. I was fanatical about it. I used to eat, drink and sleep karate. I felt as if I couldn't get enough of it. My style was wado ryu and my sensei was Walter Seaton. He was the best instructor anyone could ever have. He was so talented and certainly knew his stuff. Each week he would travel all the way from Billingham near Darlington and teach us at Warrior Street School at Walkergate in Newcastle. He was very high up in his Dan belts, well known all over and highly respected by everyone. He was strict but always fair and treated both men and women as equals.

When I was at senior school I could hardly believe that I was the same girl who stood on the dojo floor in my karate suit waiting to begin my free fighting with some of the men and women. I felt confident and as strong as an ox. I wasn't frightened of anyone and would be ready for them no matter how old, big or small they were. Yet here I am standing in the school yard allowing bullies everyday to shove and push me around; I was like putty in their hands. Some would make fun and laugh at me while others would be spitting on me and cutting small snippets of my hair. There were many other things that they said and done and not just to me. They behaved like a pack of animals and I was terrified of them. I suppose they looked upon me as this big wimp and they were right – that's exactly what I was.

Not all my school days were bad but it did affect me by jumping from one school to another. For me the best memories and part of the day at school was lunchtime – I loved my food and the meals were fantastic, everything was fresh and cooked on the premises. We always had meat and two veg. The desserts were to die for; if

nothing else it always helped to cheer me up and put a smile on
my face. My mam used to give Jackie, John and I a threepenny bit
each day for our pocket money. I used to save mine up to pay for my
karate lessons which cost one and six a week which is equal to seven
and a half pence today. My goodness, how time and money has
changed so much over the years. I had to wait quite a while before
I could afford to buy my karate suit. The price was three pounds
seventeen and six. That was a lot of money in those days. For some
folk it was a week's wages.

The October school holidays were approaching; then it was
known as potato picking week. Farmers everywhere depended on
young folk as well as adults to come and work for them during this
time. They didn't have all the big fancy tractors and machinery like
you do today. All the potatoes had to be picked by hand. I asked my
Mam can I go and do that, I need the money desperately to buy my
karate suit and I'd be paid three pounds at the end of the week. She
agreed. I was so pleased and I couldn't wait to start.

We were all picked up at the top shops on our estate in a big
open-back pickup truck. I was still very much a tomboy always
wearing trousers and had short hair. We all sat down on the
hard, dirty floor; it was great – everyone was so jolly and enjoying
themselves. The sun was shining as it was a red hot day. As the truck
drove up and down the hills we were all rocking from side to side as
we went over the bumps we almost banged our heads off each other.
Nobody cared, we were all singing songs and having a whale of a
time; under the strict health and safety rules and regulations today
such a journey like that would never have been allowed.

This was the first time I had ever been to a farm before; it was all
a very new and exciting experience for me. As soon as we arrived we
were all given a very large smelly sack material apron to wear; when
tied around our waist it almost reached the ground. We all stood
in straight lines stretching from one end of the field to the other.
There would be about seven or eight rows formed leaving enough

room between each one for the tractor to drive up and down. At the back of the tractor the rotavator would dig up all the potatoes leaving them lying on top of the soil for us all to pick. Down on our knees we went picking up as many and as quickly as we could, placing them into the middle of our aprons. We'd then grab each corner of our aprons to form a bucket shape and run quickly with them, pouring the potatoes into a big trough – and then back to the grindstone we went.

It was hard work and back breaking, but what fun we had. It was a marvellous experience and I have no regrets. But most of all the hard work had paid off – I had almost raised the amount of money I needed to buy my karate suit. But I was still short of seventeen and six, that's equal to seventy five pence today which is nothing these days, but back then it was a lot of money. As I mentioned earlier we were all given a threepenny bit each day to buy sweets with but if I was to raise the amount needed I would have to do without them for over seven and a half weeks. I was so thrilled when my Aunt Florrie and Uncle Gordon had offered to give me the extra money that I needed. I was totally gobsmacked and didn't expect it, but they knew just how much I appreciated everything they had done.

They also did karate along with their young son Kevin. Over the next three and a half years I had come a long way in karate and had passed many of my grades; each grade represented a different coloured belt and there would be nine I would have to pass before reaching my Black Belt first Dan. The grades varied between times – the higher the belt the longer it took and the more difficult it became. My main ambition was always to reach my black belt in karate no matter how long it took. Just as well we can't see into the future and know what lies ahead for us.

Chapter 12

Raymond's month's trial for his new job has almost come to an end. For us it has felt like the longest month on record. Raymond thinks he has done enough to prove himself but let's hope the management think the same. Up to now they haven't given anything away. I suppose they can't afford to make any mistakes and have to make sure they choose the right person for the job.

Although Raymond was desperate to get the position, disability or no disability he didn't want anyone bending the rules or doing him any favours and giving him the job out of sympathy. He only wanted it on his merits and his merits alone.

Well today's the day when Raymond will find out whether he's being kept on or not. "Don't worry about anything," he kept telling me before he left. "Everything's going to be fine. I can feel it. You'll see."

I wish I had as much faith as he did, I kept telling myself over and over. It was lunchtime and there was a knock at the door; it was Raymond. My heart sank and my immediate reaction was *he obviously hasn't got the job and has been sent home.* But how wrong I was – apparently he had passed with flying colours and he couldn't wait any longer to tell me the news so he came up in his dinner hour. We were both so elated and hugging and kissing each other with excitement. We could now make plans for our future together. He made quite good wages. His basic rate before his off takes was approximately nineteen pounds a week. There was always plenty of overtime of which he always took the opportunity. He was a damn good grafter. He worked with a fantastic bunch of guys and most days at lunchtime they would go outside to have a game of football and guess who was always in goal – Raymond. On a few occasions

Raymond asked my dad if he would bring me down to the factory
at lunchtime to meet the lads and to stay for the football match.
They were all as daft as a brush, full of fun and great to be with and
despite Raymond's disability he was accepted as one of the lads, he
was treated no different to anyone else and that's the way he wanted
it. The game would begin; there was certainly no exceptions or
punches pulled. They would wham the ball in as hard as they could
for Raymond to save. He would often dive too late or go to the
wrong side altogether and miss the ball completely. The lads would
shout out, "Hey jock! How the fucking hell did you miss that one?
You'd think you were blind or something. I think you need to go
and get your eyes tested after letting a goal like that in!"

Raymond was well respected by his work mates as well as the
management because he accepted everything that was said and
thrown his way without any offence taken. But he could certainly
give out as good as he got.

Raymond settled in well with the rest of the family. He was very
easy going and had a good relationship with my dad. They went out
together every Sunday morning to the Sunniside Club for a pint.
Nobody liked a pint more than Raymond did, along with a wee nip
of whisky or Drambuie. My dad was mainly a Brown Ale drinker,
like my mam. He also loved a whisky and a Drambuie and boy could
he put them away – but he could also take it. You never saw him
drunk, just happy. My dad was very popular and well liked; all the
woman loved him, and thought he was tall, dark and handsome
as well as being charming – which he was. They would come back
from the club full of the joys of spring giving us all the running
commentary of their morning out while cracking jokes over Sunday
lunch then they would lie down and have forty winks. It used to bug
my mam at the thought of my dad going out for a drink without her,
most probably from a guilty conscience more than anything else in
case he was talking about her to others but most of all with her not
being there she wouldn't be the belle of the ball and the centre of

attention as usual. I loved Raymond living down here; we thought ourselves so lucky being able to see each other every day.

I missed it so much not going back to Edinburgh on a regular basis to see his family though – goodness knows how Raymond must have been feeling. It was impossible to do because of his work so we would have to wait until the end of July when he broke up for his holidays. As far as I was concerned it couldn't come quick enough as I couldn't wait to get away from here for a break. My mam had started bullying me again. She had me all on edge and my head was buzzing. I kept wishing that she would leave me alone. It was just too good to be true: she had been too nice for too long to me especially over these last six weeks since Raymond's been here. I thought she had changed; maybe I was hoping – how wrong I was.

All of a sudden everything began to make sense. I must have been a fool and stupid enough to have believed that my mam had invited Raymond down here to make me happy, and to help to give us a start in life. I don't think so! She knew exactly what she was doing. It had all been carefully planned. At first she seemed overjoyed that I had met someone. Maybe it was all an act, who knows? I suppose what was really eating her away and rattling her cage is that she never expected or thought for one minute that Raymond and I would have fallen head over heels in love with each other and in such a short period of time we would be planning our engagement. I don't know how many times she tried to get me to break it off with him along with the terrible things that she kept saying about Raymond's mam and his family. I loved staying with them. They were the most honest, genuine, caring and loving family you could have ever wished to meet. I loved them all, especially his mam; she was an angel and I enjoyed being in her presence.

Also the things she kept saying about Raymond, there was no need. He was good to me and my mam and dad. Whenever I had gone to Edinburgh to see Raymond I would never look forward to coming back home as I never knew what frame of mind my mam was going to be in. She was like a dog with a bone, gnawing and chewing at you all the time, never knowing when to stop.

The bottom line was, she was so jealous and green with envy she couldn't bear to see me happy and especially knowing that someone loved me as much as Raymond did.

My mam would've panicked and been furious with me if I had've decided to live in Edinburgh. She wouldn't have had a skivvy to bring and fetch, clean the house, wash the windows and everything else she could think of. I was also her babysitter as Kerry was almost eight years younger than me, Laurie was nine and a half and Robert fourteen years but that didn't bother me. I enjoyed looking after them, but the biggest and most important thing of all she would've missed was not me but the money. She kept most of mine and took almost half of Raymond's and John's wages for their board which was eight pound a week. In 1973 that was a lot of money then and she was certainly making sure that she was going to get her share and more.

Chapter 13

When I was a paper girl at Redheugh Road from the age of ten, my mam was exactly the same: greedy for money. Billy Gallon was my boss. He worked from his home with his brother Bobby in the next street from where we lived. It may have been home to them but to me it was the most dirtiest place I had ever seen. It looked just like a rundown derelict shack of a place and it stunk. It was a downstairs flat and the room they worked from was straight in off the front street. The door was never closed, so that everybody passing could see them at work. It was dark and dingy with bare floorboards that looked rotten. There was nothing else in the room but this old, large wooden table that stood in the middle of the floor. This is where all the papers went on to be sorted out. Bobby was a slight cripple, one leg was shorter than the other and he limped badly. Billy was much worse: his legs were very bad. He couldn't walk anywhere without holding on to something. His whole body, head and arms seemed to shake all the time and I always thought he was going to fall over at any minute. He would be about five foot five inches tall, very thin, unshaven, no teeth, a cap on his head and wore a long filthy mac of some kind that just looked like the one that Fagin wore in Oliver Twist. He was filthy and smelly as if he hadn't been washed from one year to the other and gave me the creeps.

I had to report every night straight from school and also on Saturday afternoons and on Sunday mornings from ten o'clock until two in the afternoon where we would always finish off standing outside the Five Wands Mill Inn pub on Bensham Bank. Billy was so bad at walking that I had to go around with him to deliver the papers. He used a very large, old Silver Cross pram to put them in so he could hold on to the handle bar for balance. It took ages to fill up as it held hundreds of newspapers.

Our paper round was huge as we delivered to dozens of different streets. We started at Redheugh Road then to Marion Street, up Bank Street too School Street, around Coatsworth Road area, then back down to Bensham covering First, Second, Third and Fourth Street, down to Leasham Lane area, then coming back along Sidney Grove. Many of the old streets and banks were very steep in those days and boy was it hard work pushing and manoeuvring the pram while Billy was hanging on to it dragging his legs and bouncing all over the place. He would stand with the pram while I ran and put the papers through the letter boxes. It would take at least three hours, sometimes longer depending on the weather.

The winter time was the worst and more dangerous. By lad, did we have some lucky escapes with that pram! I used to be freezing, the snow was always deep and thick then and my mam couldn't always afford to buy us a winter coat so I would still be wearing my thin summer Burberry. My socks would never stay up as they kept falling to the bottom of my wellies while the snow and slush would be finding their way in, leaving big red rings around my legs. Then the wet and cold would be blowing up my skirt leaving the tops of my legs chapped and thick of keens, which was always very painful. My mam used to knit all our jumpers, cardigans, hats and scarves. I'll never forget the bright yellow balaclava she knitted me for the winter and always made me wear. It came right down covering the front and back of my neck and spread out almost reaching my shoulders. I just looked like Ivanhoe or one of the Sheriff of Nottingham's soldiers out of Robin Hood and his merry men. What a prat I must've looked, but there was one consolation – I certainly wouldn't have been missed in the dark.

It was certainly hard work and the biggest headache was when I had to try and push this big ruddy old pram up the bank in the snow, especially when Billy was hanging over the long handlebar of the pram. He couldn't quite keep his feet on the ground. No wonder because he had his shoes wrapped up in big sheets of polythene that went right up to his knees and were stuck on with sellotape and elastic bands to help keep his feet dry. Just as well I was strong because by the time I reached the top of the bank I must have looked as red as a cockerel. The sweat would be running off me, but the biggest nightmare of all was when we had to come back down again. The skier Eddie the Eagle didn't have a look in. We must've nearly broken his record. One minute we were at the top and, within a flash, at the bottom. That pram just didn't glide down – it bounced most of the way because it was so highly sprung. Poor Billy, he just looked like a puppet on strings and nearly ended up inside the pram a couple of times. I would be gritting my teeth and hanging on for grim death. How we never caused an accident on the way down or injured ourselves I'll never know. At the time I was terrified but looking back if anyone had been watching they would probably think we were rehearsing for a comedy show.

So after all of that my pay at the end of the week was only twenty-one and six. Today that's equal to one pound and twelve and a half pence and my mam kept it all giving me nothing back. Just as well some were kind enough to give me a small tip sometimes, which I was always thankful for and allowed to keep.

My twin brother John and I were always close as children. From the age of nine he fell into a terrible habit of playing with matches and fireworks. I think it was very much a boy's thing. My mam had me acting like a little private detective, spying and following him everywhere, unbeknown to him of course, to make sure he wasn't spending his pocket money on buying bangers or any other fireworks he could get his hands on and to report back if he was.

I'll never forget the day when he was almost ten years old; he came into the house screaming. I don't know how he managed to get home – maybe someone else had brought him, I don't know. All I remember was when he opened the kitchen door and I saw the state his face was in I went into shock myself. I was screaming, jumping up and down and running around the room like a headless chicken with fear because I thought he was going to die. The front of his hair was burnt, he had no eyebrows or eyelashes, the pupils of his eyes had disappeared leaving only the whites showing and his face was as black as anything. Apparently he had lit a banger and threw it away. He had waited and because it hadn't gone off he decided to go over and pick it up, turned it towards his face thinking it must have gone out when it exploded.

That's how it all happens, quick as a flash and as easy as that he was rushed by an ambulance to Walkergate eye infirmary in Newcastle which was a specialist hospital dealing with many different types of eye problems, injuries and emergencies. Children weren't allowed as visitors in hospitals in those days but every time my mam went in to see him I always made sure she took me with her. John's bed was on the ground floor by the window. Sometimes it would be pouring down with rain and I would be soaking wet with standing outside, but I didn't care because it was so important for me to see him just to know that he was alright even if it was just looking at the back of his head through the window. I missed him so much.

My mam would tell him I was there and he always turned around, gave me a big smile and waved. I used to cry when I saw his eyes bandaged up, with big pads on them. I was terrified in case he would never see again. I've often looked back and thought how dreadful it would have been not just for John and me but also for my mam and dad, if we had both ended up being blind. How spooky and weird would that have been, especially with us being twins? I am a great believer in fate and what will be, will be. It was John's long eyelashes that saved his sight. Thank goodness he made a full recovery.

It wasn't all doom and gloom at Redheugh Road. I still have many happy memories of living there, especially leading up to

Christmas. Each year my mam would buy new packs of different coloured crepe paper for us to make Christmas decorations with. We would cut them into long strips about six inches wide, then John and I would take an end each and twist them into lovely spiral streamers and hang them across the ceilings and walls. We also made our own Christmas lanterns from white sheets of paper, then we would colour them in with crayons. We would then slot them onto a long piece of string and hang them across the room from one corner to the other. Many people had to do that then as Christmas decorations were so expensive to buy, but making our own was so much better, as we had a lot of fun doing them.

I used to love looking in the local corner shop windows. They were all beautifully dressed up and really Christmassy. The highlight was always when my mam took us to Woolworths or Shepherds in Gateshead, which was always known as the biggest and the best store – and it most certainly was. Leading up to Christmas there used to be this brilliant advert shown on TV about Shepherds. You couldn't help but sing along as the words and music were so jolly and catchy. They showed you all the different departments and the fantastic gifts and toys you could buy. It always put me into the Christmas spirit and made me feel so happy and excited. The toy department was upstairs where Father Christmas was. It was absolutely huge and filled with nothing else but toys. Each year they always had this large train set that travelled around the whole of the shop which was set up above for all the public to see. I found it all so magical and breathtaking.

My mam and dad were members of the RAFA (Royal Air Force Association) club in Gateshead. They held a Christmas party each year and we always had a great time. I always loved it when we danced to the 'Grand Old Duke of York' as it was my favourite and we always received a lovely present at the end, but the most exciting and best Christmas party we ever went to was at Signum Pumps, the factory where my dad worked on the Team Valley Trading Estate in Gateshead. They knew how to party big style. There had to be at least 150 to 200 children there. I used to feel like the bee's knees with my new dress on, as it wasn't very often that I got a new dress of my own to wear. But at Christmas time it was always a very special occasion to get one. We would be there all afternoon, partying, having fun and playing games.

When it was time to eat we all had to line up in big queues; it was very well organised. There were long rows of tables stretching from one end of the room to the other, with white tablecloths on. There was dozens and dozens of plates filled with sausage rolls, cream cakes, sandwiches, crisps – you name it, it was there. We all started off with jelly and custard and cups of juice. To me it was like being at the Ritz. After we finished our food we were then taken into another huge room that was filled with rows and rows of chairs and a big projector screen where we watched lots of different cartoons.

To finish off the day we went back to the big hall where there was a live band waiting to entertain us. One year the group was called The Silver Dollars – they were fantastic and I think they were a local boy band. The only song I can remember them singing was called Rainbow, which later on they recorded and I believe it went to number one in the charts. It was a brilliant song and one of my mam's favourites. When she bought the record, I played it over and over again. Even today I personally feel it is one of the best records ever released.

We always finished the afternoon off with a twisting competition. The twist and the shake were all the rage back then in the sixties. There was this one particular boy who won every year; he would only be about nine or ten. He was a right little star and just looked like a little mini Elvis – and boy could he move. We all ended up forming a large circle and clapped and cheered him on. He literally danced around covering the whole of the floor and was anything but shy – you could tell he was enjoying every minute of it. He was a well deserved winner and always received a fantastic prize.

At the end of the party everyone received a brilliant present and also a big bag of goodies. It must have cost the company a fortune to put the party on, but we all went home very happy and had a marvellous time. I have always loved Christmas and still do today, but when you are young and a child and still believe in Father Christmas there is just something extra special and magical about it, isn't there?

At Redheugh we had open fires – most of the houses did back then. We had one downstairs in the kitchen and the other one was upstairs in our bedroom in the attic where we slept. It was only on Christmas Eve when my dad would bank the fire up in our bedroom and set it alight. He knew we would be awake the best part of the night, but at least we would be warm.

We would always have to be in bed extra early on Christmas Eve. John and I would be in and out of bed as many times looking out of the large attic window, which overlooked the roof tops and right along Redheugh Road. Nine times out of ten it would be snowing and everywhere just looked like fairyland. We were hoping to catch a glimpse of Santa on his sleigh in the sky. I used to love the smell of the open fire – it would be crackling and burning bright and as the flames flickered it would send shadows right across the ceiling and the walls. It made the whole room look so cosy and warm.

For me Christmas Eve was the most exciting night ever. We kept quietly creeping to the top of the stairs, listening to make sure everyone was in bed fast asleep before going down to see if any presents had been left. Sometimes it would only be two or three in the morning but we couldn't wait any longer. My older sister Jackie would join us as we quietly crept one behind the other down the long staircase trying very hard not to make a sound as Kerry and Laurie were still babies and we didn't want to wake them up. Our presents were always in the kitchen inside a white pillowcase; we always knew which ones were ours, as they were put in the same place every year. We may not have got the biggest and best presents compared to many other children but that didn't matter to us, not one little bit, as there was five of us to buy for.

We always had a great Christmas and my mam and dad always did us proud. We were always thrilled with what we got and never disappointed. They always made sure we had more than enough no matter what circumstances they may have been in. Just after the age of twelve someone decided to spoil everything for me by telling me that Father Christmas wasn't real. I was devastated. At least we were children for much longer then, but how things have changed since I was young. Christmas is certainly not what it used to be; it is now far too commercial and has lost the meaning of what it is all about. How sad. We as parents and grandparents owe it to our children and grandchildren to keep the magic and true meaning of Christmas real and alive for our future generations.

Chapter 14

How time flies! The years seem to go by so quickly – it is now
Christmas 1973 and Raymond and I have already been engaged for
one year. That same Christmas we set our wedding day for June 20th
1976, on Raymond's twenty-fifth birthday. It wasn't until much later
that we realised it was a leap year and that date fell on a Sunday.
Unfortunately you never heard of marriages taking place on
Sundays back then. So we had to bring it forward to the Saturday,
which was a little disappointing but there was nothing we could do
about it. We were so lucky that Saturday the nineteenth was still
available at the church and also with our caterers, car hire and
photography etc.

I was the first to be married in white in our family. I wanted
it to be a big special occasion because it's not every day you get
married, is it? This had always been my dream and also to have
children – I couldn't wait. When I told my mam her immediate
reaction was "well don't expect any help from us, we can't afford it.
If that's what you want then you can pay for it". She certainly always
knew how to put the damper on something. My dad never had any
say in the matter as she ruled the roost. She knew fine well that we
didn't expect her to pay for it all. To be honest we weren't looking
for anything and were quite happy to do it ourselves, but my mam
was the one who had told me to give her plenty of notice of our
wedding day so that she could start and put some money away on a
regular basis to help towards it – as usual she went back on her word
and let me down once again, even though there were still two and
a half years to go. It was only two pounds a week that she said she
needed to put away so it wasn't as if she couldn't afford it, as she was
raking it in from us as well as John and my Dad and had more than

enough to do it.

I couldn't help but feel that my mam had made it quite clear what I meant to her and also my marriage: nothing!

We both knew that the next two and a half years were going to be tough because it now meant we would have to put away as much money as we could possibly afford each week. Not just for the wedding but also to build up our bottom drawer (meaning buying household goods to put away). Then we hoped to find a flat or a house somewhere for us to rent which would also need to be carpeted and furnished. Not forgetting our honeymoon – that's if we had any money left.

As time went by my mam made our lives not just a misery but also as difficult as she possibly could for us saving up for our wedding day. There was always something that she wanted money off us for. I have never known anyone to be so greedy and selfish – she was a total control freak and she certainly controlled me and my dad, but we were daft and stupid enough to have allowed her to do it. What Jean wanted, Jean always got, no matter whom she hurt or upset in the process of doing it; as long as she got her own way, that's all that mattered.

Chapter 15

I would be about seventeen and a half when I was given my first guitar from a guy who drank with my mam and dad at the Rose, Shamrock and Thistle. I remember meeting him on a few occasions myself when I was there. He had the most infectious and dirtiest laugh I had ever heard, a real happy go lucky guy. He was described to me as very Mexican looking with shoulder length dark wavy hair and a droopy moustache. His name was Alan but he was known to everyone as Speedy.

One day out of the blue he arrived at our house and kindly gave me one of his oldest and fondest guitars. It was a small Suzuki guitar. Apparently they were great friends and had travelled everywhere together. I was absolutely thrilled and felt so privileged that he had chosen me to give his special guitar to. He then tuned it and began to sing and play 'House of the rising sun'. He sounded fantastic and made the guitar talk. It had the most beautiful sound to it and I couldn't believe it was now mine.

Speedy also left my mam a notepad explaining about the chords and frets I needed to use. He also drew some simple pictures showing where my fingers had to be placed and numbered them. I was that excited I couldn't wait to start and practise. I knew nothing about music or guitars and realised it wasn't going to be that easy to learn. My mam promised Speedy that she would help me and she did at first, but as usual I knew it wouldn't last for long. Apparently I was keeping her from more important and better things than sitting around and helping me. She wasn't interested, found it boring and couldn't be bothered any more.

Although I found it difficult I was enjoying it so much and didn't want to give up. At first I practised on three chords over and over again, day in, day out. Although I still struggled I was determined to succeed and get it right; all I needed was some help, guidance and encouragement. I was so desperate to achieve playing the guitar – not to be brilliant or clever at it, just enough to get me by.

I had been playing it for a few months now, or should I say trying to play if you know what I mean. My mam and dad decided to go shopping this one day meaning I had the house to myself, so I decided that me and my guitar would sit on the front step and strum away in the sunshine. Then all of a sudden I heard a voice say, "That's not quite right, Christine, there are parts you're playing wrong."

At first I wasn't too sure who it was then all of a sudden he spoke again. "Hi Christine, it's just me, Tommy Orton from over the road."

He lived in Coanwood Gardens which was the cul-de-sac opposite us. I felt so embarrassed and stupid about what he had just said even though I knew he was right, but I was so thrilled that he had taken the time to stop and speak. I had known him for years; he was a lovely lad, quietly spoken, about five feet six inches tall, slim build with light brown hair. He was quite good looking; I always fancied him. You know what it's like when you're kids – you have crushes on people. When I could see, what attracted me to Tommy more than anything else was his lovely smile. I never knew him very well as he didn't play with any of us in the street. Maybe his friends lived elsewhere. To me he always appeared to be a very quiet and shy person but he would never pass you in the street without giving you a smile, a wink or saying hello, which always made my day. He had two sisters who were much older than him, Vera and Mary. I knew them much better as they always stopped to talk to my mam and dad when they were in the garden. Vera worked at Irons which was our local hardware shop in the next street. Everyone knew her well; sometimes she would pop into ours for a cup of coffee and a chat. Nobody anywhere could mistake

Vera's husky and chirpy voice and also her dirty laugh, it was very infectious.

Then Tommy spoke again, "I play the guitar, Christine. If you would like any help I'll teach you, I don't mind."

I couldn't believe my luck, I was thrilled to ribbons. No need to guess what my answer was and how I managed to restrain my emotions, I'll never know. I felt like putting my hands up like Macho Man and shouting "yes, get in" and giving him the biggest hug ever. I already mentioned I didn't know very much about him – it was the biggest surprise ever... now those are the types of surprises that I like.

He wasted no time and more or less started to teach me straight away. I found it much easier and more enjoyable learning the guitar especially when someone was showing you on a one-to-one basis. I kept improving all the time; everything seemed to be coming together and I was now able to sing and play a couple of songs on my own. Nothing fancy or flash, just plain and simple, and I remember being so pleased with myself and so was Tommy. He was great. He always had a lovely way of explaining and showing you how to do something. It just goes to show what you can do and achieve in a matter of months with determination but more so when someone takes an interest in what you are doing and offers a helping hand, gives you guidance and lots of encouragement through life – that can take you a long long way and it certainly did with me. I have never seen Tommy since then and hope to bump into him one day. Maybe we could get our guitars out and do a duo together – that would be good fun.

When I eventually became more confident in playing the guitar I managed to pick up six or seven songs that I could sing and play too. They were mainly ballads and a couple of them were country and western. I didn't have a clue about music and still don't today. I have never been one to understand or even to play in the correct bars, beats or rhythms like others do. I found it all too difficult so I just developed my own way and style because that is the only way I could manage. I was never brilliant but always knew enough to get me by. To me that's all that mattered.

Chapter 16

One day in spring in 1973 I can't remember why or how it came about but I ended up taking my guitar into the Fountain View Centre for the first time. We all had a sing-along in the room where I worked. Within no time members from the other two work rooms came in to see what was going on and also joined in. It was also the first time I had ever sang in front of an audience and was so pleased that I hadn't made any mistakes. Who would've ever thought for one minute that taking my guitar in and singing that day would've opened doors to my music?

Mary Davidson who was deputy manager there was very surprised when she heard me sing and also expressed how much she enjoyed it and wondered why I hadn't brought my guitar in before now. She then asked if I would do it all over again so her husband Tom could hear me. Apparently he was manager of the Dragoni Brothers who were a very popular and well known music band in those days. Since 1966 they had performed and entertained at many charity events across the North East.

As promised Tom came in to hear me the following day. He expressed how much he liked my voice and also the songs I sang and played. He knew I was nervous and put me at ease with his jolly and chirpy voice. He was a lovely man. He then asked me if I would be interested in singing at some of his charity shows that he had lined up for the Dragoni Brothers. I could hardly believe that Tom was asking me, plain little me. I was so shocked and blown away that you could've knocked me over with a feather. I was that excited I could hardly get to sleep at night for just thinking about it.

There were four of them in the band: two were Dragone brothers, Michael on keyboard and Joe on the accordion; John

Valente, their brother in law, played the mandolin and Frank Tatoli, their friend, was on the drums. Whenever they played you always knew you were in for a marvellous night; no one ever went home disappointed.

It wasn't until 1972 that the Dragoni Brothers approached Tom Davidson asking him to become their manager. At the time he felt it was a massive task as he had no experience in 'showbiz' but Tom was one of those guys who was always up for a challenge, no matter what it may be, and this was no exception. Tom's passion and goal in life, as was the Dragoni Brothers', was always about wanting to help as many people as they possibly could, especially those who were less fortunate than themselves. Tom went to seek some help and advice from a local priest he knew. His name was Father Tom Cass. He was very well known, loved and respected by everyone – not just from those in the Catholic faith but also those outside it. He was also a very charming, wise and knowledgeable man who sadly died some years ago.

He had arranged successful big charity events himself, which were mainly held at the Mayfair in Newcastle, so if anyone could help Tom it would certainly be him. He spoke some very simple words to Tom that day but very powerful and profound ones which were 'to always go big in what you do in life, think big, aim big and don't look back'. Tom thrived on those words and put them into action immediately. Within two years the Dragoni Brothers became bigger than ever, their shows were in great demand and were a sell out wherever they went because of the huge support from their faithful fans. How fantastic is that? Their music and also their single release 'Faith of our Fathers' was often played on Radio Newcastle, one of our local radio stations that is still around today.

They were all great guys and full of fun. John Valente was always pulling my leg about something but whenever I performed at their shows – which sometimes could be huge events – Tom Davidson and the Dragonis always made me feel so welcome and would put my mind at ease straight away. They always knew how nervous I was before going out on stage. I was always told how handsome and good looking they all were. Frank was the youngest of them. The build-up before they came out on stage to perform was always exciting but as soon as they walked on waving their hands, wearing their black trousers, bright yellow silk shirts and sombreros the crowds would go wild – cheering, clapping and sending out wolf whistles. Everyone thought that Frankie was drop-dead gorgeous with his shoulder-length dark hair and droopy moustache, but most of all his big smile. The girls would all be shouting out his name.

In the spring of 1974 the Dragoni Brothers were about to face their biggest challenge ever – and in saying that so was I. Tom never let go of those wonderful inspirational words of wisdom from Father Tom Cass. He continued to think big, aim big and never looked back. So... he stepped out in faith, went ahead and booked the City Hall in Newcastle. Although the City Hall is still well used today by many celebs along with the enormous Newcastle Arena, back then this was the biggest and real I am place to be, where all the big stars appeared such as Cliff Richards, Slade and Status Quo.

It was a massive venue – the exact number of seats it held was 2133. Can you imagine filling that amount? But because this was a private booking and private function it meant that Tom would be totally responsible for the sale of all the tickets, not forgetting the amount of artists he needed to find as well as arranging the show from beginning to end. Tom knew that there was a tremendous amount of hard work involved as always, but for a project and performance as big as this it was going to be much harder than ever before. I wonder if some thought he was being too adventurous or maybe had bitten off more than he could chew this time, but because Tom had so much faith and support from his fantastic team of young local helpers, family, friends, his devoted wife Mary, not forgetting the many local artists who also gave their time freely over and over again, and finally the biggest idols of them all who dedicated so much of their time and effort – the Dragoni Brothers. How could anyone fail with such tremendous support like that behind them?

Tom was practically on his knees by the time he had finished and also was on a high. Who could've blamed him as he pulled it off big style – and I mean big style! Altogether 2,240 tickets were sold, so they had to put on stage an overflow of 107 seats. How awesome, outstanding and brilliant was that?

When the big day arrived it was a real experience for me meeting so many other artists backstage in the changing rooms. I wore a long, loose, sleeveless, satin black dress with small printed multi coloured diamond shapes on it. My hair was long then, with my fringe taken back off my face. Frank Wappat, one of our local DJs, was our compère for the evening. Tom gave me a ten minute slot – enough time to sing three songs. When I was taken on stage I found it nerve-racking, breathtaking, moving and exciting all at the same time. It was like a dream. I could hardly believe that it was me standing on that stage and especially at the City Hall, in front of 2240 people, performing on my own.

The audience welcomed me by clapping which helped me to relax and focus on what I had to do. I do feel that the biggest advantage for me that night, which I know helped to get me through, was the fact of my not being able to see, otherwise I am certain the outcome would've been much different. So it just goes to show how even the loss of something can have its benefits, as it can work both ways. The show was a huge success, mega to be exact. My idols and everyone else's, the Dragoni Brothers, were top of the bill as always. They literally blew everyone away; I had never experienced anything like it before. They had the whole place up on its feet, clapping, singing and dancing up and down the aisles and even on the stage. They played a very special brand of music – I am sure that this was the secret and key to their huge success. It was so inspirational, uplifting and exciting that it couldn't help but capture the audience as it made you feel so happy and jolly inside, it really touched your soul; I know it did with me. As far as I'm concerned, and I'm sure that many others would have agreed, the Dragonis put on as big a show if not even better than some of your big stars back then and even today! It is also a fact that the Dragoni Brothers that night had sold more tickets than even some of the big celeb concerts that had performed there over the years.

The following two years they had topped the bill again at the City Hall, Newcastle and also had topped the bill at the Empire Theatre, Sunderland as well as the Mayfair Dance Hall in Newcastle – but as the saying goes all good things must come to an end. Tom Davidson and the Dragoni Brothers retired in 1983. Over the seventeen years from all the hard work and dedication from the Dragonis, Tom and their own special team of young helpers and volunteers from the Saint Theresa's Club together raised tens of thousands of pounds which went to help provide a better quality of life for local handicapped children and their families. It also went towards buying special ambulance buses to take the handicapped children away on holidays and also trips to Lourdes in France. They also helped to purchase and provide many pieces of specialised equipment for local hospitals and give to Cancer Research. To be honest there is a list as long as your arm but unfortunately too many to mention.

What a wonderful legacy they have left behind for us all to remember. Finally I would like to say I feel so privileged and honoured to have been just a small part of the Dragonis' life and for the most memorable and fantastic ten years I appeared at some of their shows, both big and small. Also to Tom for believing in me that day and giving me the opportunity to fulfill my dream in something that I loved and always wanted to do. Together the encouragement and confidence I gained from all of you has helped me through life more than you will ever know. Thank you.

Chapter 17

Although I absolutely loved singing, my love and passion for karate was just as great but I found it very hard to accept that my karate days were over. I had been totally obsessed about reaching my black belt, never thinking for one minute that something like losing my sight would have ever happened to me. I knew deep down that I was still bitter because I felt totally robbed of my dream and ambition and couldn't get it out of my mind, but because my mam had such a huge living room – and I mean huge – it meant that I could still practise my karate. When the armchairs were moved out of the way there was certainly more than enough room for me to practise.

As soon as I put my karate suit on it was strange how different it made me feel. I became much happier within myself and forgot about everything else. I know it might sound daft but somehow it helped to make me feel whole and normal again, even if it was just for a short period of time, it was amazing. Raymond had always been my rock, encourager and biggest supporter in everything I had ever done. Whenever I had doubts or negative thoughts in my mind – and believe you me there were many back then – somehow he always managed to make me pick myself up and to turn my thoughts into more positive ones. He made me feel more confident, happier and better about myself, which sometimes for me wasn't always easy to do.

I would have been about nineteen and a half when all of a sudden one day Raymond spurted out: "Have you ever given it much thought about going back to karate?"

I was gobsmacked, quite hurt and upset about his stupid and ridiculous remarks because of all people I thought he should have known better than anyone else to come out with something like that. However he was deadly serious and couldn't understand why I was making such a fuss about it all. He then spoke in quite a stern voice and reminded me about the number of times I moaned and groaned about how much I loved and missed doing karate and that all I ever wanted to do was to achieve my black belt. Then he would say, "If that's the case why don't you get up and do something about it? Because if you're quite happy to sit back and let your blindness defeat, rule and ruin your life forever, then that's up to you and fine by me, but don't expect me to do the same!"

He certainly didn't pull any punches that particular day and I can assure you I was not a happy bunny. I thought *who the hell does he think he's talking to?* At that particular time I always thought that it was Raymond who was walking around with this great big chip on his shoulders and was in denial of his disability because he was so strong-willed about everything and adamant that he wasn't going to let anyone or anything get in his way and stop him from doing something. "I'm just as good, normal and capable as the next guy, there's nowt wrong with me," he would always say. But how wrong I was. It was then that I realised that it was me who had the mega problem and not him. Sometimes we need to hear some home truths about ourselves in order to help us become unstuck. In other words, free us from our fears, anxiety, feelings of worthless and helplessness and so on, even if it does hurt and we don't want to hear it or believe it.

Once again it made me sit down and take another good look at myself, meaning reflecting back over the last few years. Was I just kidding myself into thinking that everything was okay or was I still feeling very bitter and sorry for myself about what had happened to me and just not quite knowing how to let go and move forward? Maybe I was just spending too much time thinking negative thoughts about myself. Raymond was dead right – after all, I was the one who said I was determined to go out there and make my mark in life, but once again I still hadn't done anything about it. Why did

I keep allowing myself to fall back into a rut? Isn't it so easy to do? I knew it was down to me, and only me, to make myself get up and do something about it and because of the way I was feeling in my heart I knew that if I was to achieve all that I wanted to I would have to once again give my mind another real good talking too.

You may laugh and think how stupid is that, but believe you me it really does work. I am being very serious when I say this, as you know I wasn't the brightest or cleverest of people but I did come to realise that whenever I fed my brain with more cheerful, inspiring and positive thoughts I noticed the change in me straight away. My mind would become much clearer and I could think better as I definitely felt this buzz of energy come inside me from somewhere. It made me feel wow, happy and more positive inside that I would jump upon my feet and say out loud, "Right Christine, this is it, the end of all talking, it's now time to get the whip cracking and put things into action".

This was probably the first time that I truly began to believe in myself more and when I say this I mean truly believing in myself. This is something that I feel we all need to do. If we long to reach our dreams and goals in life whatever they may be, disability or no disability, all I am going to say is don't let anything or anyone dampen your morale and stand in the way of reaching them. Obviously we have to be sensible about what it is and always know our limitations. Throughout life for me this has been the only way I have managed to conquer and to achieve so many things by using my own methods and positive thinking. Remember it doesn't just happen overnight – sometimes it can take many long months if not even years of hard work and determination before we reach what we are aiming for, but believe you me the satisfaction and the feeling you receive along the way by doing it and especially succeeding in getting there is second to none.

You already know what my dreams and goals were – that's right, to reach my black belt in karate – well you will just have to read further on to see if I managed to achieve it or not and if I did when and how did I do it. You may even think to yourself that there is no way that a non-sighted person could achieve anything like that. I remember thinking exactly the same when I heard of non-sighted football and cricket teams: – how on earth could they possibly do it? Well only time will tell.

Chapter 18

It is 1976 and I am 22 years old. I can hardly believe that our wedding day is just a few weeks away. I was so excited and couldn't wait to become Mrs Deponio. I absolutely loved my new name to be and would be proud to carry it and be part of my new family, but most of all to have Raymond as my husband. I felt so happy and lucky to have him, I couldn't have asked for more.

My mam never believed for one minute that we would've raised the amount of money needed for our wedding day, so of course that made us more determined than ever to prove her wrong. Everything was sorted and paid for and my mam had certainly kept to her word about not helping us: she hadn't put a penny towards anything. We were just so proud of ourselves that we had done it entirely on our own and had nobody to thank for anything.

Raymond's mam was just the opposite – she was an absolute gem; she may not have had much but she would give you her last if she could. We had four bridesmaids: my sister Kerry, my cousin Kim, my niece Elaine, and Raymond's niece Adalyne. We had two page boys: my brother Robert and nephew John. We were getting married at All Saints Church which was just around the corner from where we lived. Our wedding reception was being held in the church hall next to it, which was definitely not my choice. My mam may not have paid for the wedding but she certainly made sure that she took control of everything and would have the final say, no matter what.

Again I can't believe that I was so weak, frightened and stupid enough to have allowed her to do it and she knew that. On many occasions Raymond wanted to give her a piece of his mind but I always begged him not to say anything because I would be the one who would receive all the horrible verbal abuse – and I mean horrible – and to be honest my head couldn't always take it. She always knew what strings to pull and who to pull them on: me and my dad!

By the eve of our wedding it had rained for almost six weeks, more on than off – at the time everybody including those on TV were all calling it the rainy season as they hadn't known anything quite like it before. I kept hoping and praying it would change overnight, but no matter what, I was determined that nothing was going to spoil my big day. Well at least that's what I thought.

I mainly always had short hair but since meeting Raymond I had decided to let it grow long. My hair was light brown and straight so I thought on my wedding day wouldn't it be nice to have some curls and a bit of bounce in it. So for a while I borrowed some of my mam's sponge curlers and each night I would practise putting them in and tie a scarf around to stop them from falling out. It made me feel like an old woman and I didn't manage to sleep well – goodness knows what I looked like. Well, after all that the curls never seemed to stay in for very long and as soon as they got caught in the wind they soon dropped and disappeared.

Raymond stayed overnight with his older brother at my Aunt Elsie's house – she was my dad's sister. Apparently it was bad luck for the groom to see the bride on the night before her wedding I was told. It was also a tradition and good luck to wear something old, something new, something borrowed and something blue. I don't know how many times throughout the day I kept checking to make sure everything was there in its place for tomorrow and I hadn't forgotten anything. I thought I would have an early night and I was just about to get into bed when all of a sudden there was a horrendous loud noise. I immediately went downstairs to find out what it was but my mam and dad were just in the process of opening the front door themselves to discover what had caused it. I had never ever heard rain like it and my parents remarked that the rain was coming down so hard and fast that it was like stair rods jumping back into the air about two feet off the ground. They both expressed that they had never seen anything like it before and found it quite frightening, simply because within a matter of seconds apparently all you could see were the grassy bits where the trees stood. The road and pavements had disappeared under the water and the street just looked like a proper flowing river. There was also thunder and lightning but I don't remember exactly how long it lasted – all I know was that it was really scary, like a horror movie on TV. When I eventually went back to bed my heart just sank and I couldn't stop thinking about the weather and what it was going to be like tomorrow.

As soon as I woke up the next morning the first thing I did was go downstairs and find out what the weather was like. As soon as I opened the front door the heat immediately hit me, with the sun beaming on my face – it was a miracle and amazing. It had been so long since we'd had any sunshine that you nearly forgot what it was like. My spirits were lifted up no end and there was nothing but big smiles on my face, I just couldn't believe my luck. That was the first day of the Indian summer in 1976 that we all experienced, thoroughly enjoyed and which is still spoken about today.

I wasn't getting married until two thirty in the afternoon, so it would allow plenty of time for Raymond's family coming down from Edinburgh on a minibus. Raymond's brother Michael who was fifteen months older was his best man. He was a great guy, always full of fun and as mad as a hatter. Everybody loved him as there was never a dull moment when he was around.

They all arrived about lunchtime. I was so pleased to see them and my mind was put at ease because I had been terrified that they might get lost on the way down. It wasn't until Raymond's family arrived and made such a fuss of me as usual that I felt my wedding day had begun. I was now more excited than ever because they were here as I loved them so much. They were the most wonderful people to be with and I always felt so happy and better about myself when they were around. Also the amount of beautiful presents that they gave us meant so much to us, but the best was yet to come – when our Michael and Bill went back to the minibus to bring the presents in from Raymond's mum. *What on earth could it be,* I thought as I could hear them puffing and struggling as they carried them up the garden path. What a thud it made when they plunged them down on the sitting room floor.

Once again I was so excited and I couldn't wait to get my hands on them to see what it was. My breath was literally taken away when I realised what they were – there were four pieces of the most beautiful furniture that anyone could ever wish for. I was so touched and deeply moved as no one had ever given me anything like this before. The first was a highly polished beautiful, wooden nest of tables, the larger one on the outside with four small drop leaf tables slotted on runners underneath. They were so unusual and I absolutely loved them. Next was a large white wooden ottoman with a thick padded printed cushion on top of it. It also had the most beautiful matching upholstered dressing chair to go with it. They were just magnificent and finally our Gloria, Raymond's sister, had bought us the most beautiful Queen Anne leather, buttoned stool which I also loved. Goodness knows how much it all cost – they never bought cheap; it was always the best. I could tell that these gifts had been chosen and bought with great thought, love and affection which has always meant so much to me.

My twin brother John had been courting his girlfriend Wendy for a few years. She was a local girl from Lobley Hill and all of a sudden out of the blue they decided to get married a few months prior to our wedding day. So my mam swopped the rooms back round again and I was now back in my old one above the wash house. You should have seen the state I had it in – it was like being in a warehouse. It was stocked from ceiling to floor and wall to wall with our wedding presents and also the many things that we had bought along the way for our bottom drawer. There was just enough room for me to stand and get changed and to climb into bed.

We still hadn't managed to find anywhere for us to live and it certainly wasn't for trying as we had been everywhere but there was nothing. My new B.P.R.O. Oliver Ryder and his wife Phyllis became great friends of ours and they also came to our wedding. Raymond already knew Phyllis as he used to work with her at Kavli's cheese factory. They were both disabled – Oliver had a false leg and Phyllis had one leg shorter than the other and wore a heavy built up shoe.

They were both members of the Fountain View social club and Oliver was on the committee so whenever we were down there we always made a point of sitting with them. You always knew you were in for a good night being in their company because they were both very chirpy, sociable and liked a good laugh. Phyllis was as daft as a brush, great fun and I think everyone would hear her loud voice and her dirty, husky laugh from a mile away. She was a very strong willed woman, straight as a die and smoked liked a chimney. On the other hand Oliver was much quieter but had a great sense of humour and loved nothing more than a good old chinwag as well as a laugh. In my opinion they went well together. We absolutely loved them to bits and thought very highly of them and so did everyone else.

They had two children, Linda and Neville. Linda was married to Frank and they had a little boy Paul who was gorgeous. They lived at Cemetery Road in Gateshead and had been waiting to move house for the last few months. It was an old terraced, two bedroomed, downstairs flat which had a long passageway, a small cosy sitting room with a scullery, a modernised walk in pantry, with a large bathroom and toilet and it also had a small back yard that was big enough to hang some washing out. It was church property and was rented from an agency in Newcastle.

Oliver had taken us down a couple of months prior to our wedding day to show us it as Lyne and Frank had put our names forward hoping that the agency would consider accepting us as their new tenants but he also warned us to be prepared that there could be a long waiting list and we may not be considered at all. It was a dream. We fell in love with it straight away and couldn't stop thinking about it and we lived in hope from then. The agency knew the date we were getting married and as time was ticking by we hadn't heard anything, so it didn't look as if it was going to happen. I couldn't bear the thought of starting our married life together living in with my parents but there was nothing we could do about it and would just have to carry on and make the most of it like everyone else.

So here I am back to my big day. I was so pleased when I heard my Auntie Florrie's voice – time was moving on and I needed someone to help me get dressed and also to make sure that everything was perfect and that my hair as well as myself looked fine. Well, after all it was my wedding day and as they say one of the most important days of your life. I knew that everybody's eyes would be fixed on me to see what I was wearing and what I looked like, so obviously I wanted to look my best.

The only thing that kept upsetting me all day long was the fact that I couldn't see myself or Raymond and desperately wanted to which made me feel very emotional. I knew it wasn't going to happen, so why I kept torturing myself like that I just don't know. I realised I had to snap out of it quickly and to focus on everything else because if I didn't, not only would I just ruin my day but also everyone else's and I didn't want that to happen. I was just about to slip into my wedding dress. I had tried it on many times before but this time it was for real – it was beautiful and I couldn't wait to wear it as I felt a million dollars with it on. I know I said, my wedding dress, but it really wasn't mine – I had borrowed it from my cousin Clarice who was my Aunt Elsie's daughter. She had been married a couple of years previous. I felt very embarrassed about asking her, but I explained to her that if I had had to buy my own then we wouldn't have been able to afford everything else. She was very understanding and was only too glad to help.

For the bridesmaids' dresses I chose the colour peach and because my Aunt Florrie was a dressmaker she offered to make them for me which helped to keep the costs down. The page boys wore long black trousers, a white shirt and black dickie bow tie and I heard they looked real cute and that the bridesmaids looked beautiful. When I took my curlers out, my hair dropped down and went into lovely, long ringlets. "Leave them like that," my Aunt Florrie said, "don't comb them through, I'll just gently prise them apart and loosen them up slightly, as they look lovely and I don't want to spoil them."

Then she went into her handbag and said, "I'm just going to put a little bit of make-up on you."

I had never worn make up before and made it quite clear that I wasn't going to start now. "But you have to, today of all days," she kept saying. "Just a little blusher, eye shadow and some lipstick, that's all, nothing else."

Make-up was definitely not for me. I couldn't imagine myself wearing it, more so now with not being able to see as I was terrified in case she made me look like a baby doll. She was a very strong-willed person and was making sure she was going to get her own way, do or die. I know that she had my best interests at heart, but there was no way out so I had to give in.

As soon as she finished she had to dash away because time was getting on and I would be leaving very shortly myself. All of a sudden I remembered I hadn't put my blue garter on because it was impossible for me to do it on my own without falling over as there were many layers of netting to get through. I then heard my older sister Gina outside on the landing talking to her husband Alex, so I went to ask if she could do it for me. She laughed and said to Alex, "How about you doing her the honour?"

"With pleasure," he said in his lovely deep Scottish accent. He was more like my big brother than a brother in law as he had seen me grow up since the age of ten or eleven. His main language was Gaelic as he came from the Isle of Lewis, from Stornoway, in the Outer Hebrides. I once spent six weeks there living with his parents, family and my sister Gina while Alex worked away. The family were lovely and I got on well with all of them. They lived in a very large bungalow in the heart of the country with some land attached. It was a beautiful place to live and many of the locals didn't speak English. Alex quite often called me Kirsty instead of Christine with him being Scottish Gaelic. I loved the way he pronounced the name; it was the way he rolled his 'Rs' and I always said if I ever met a Scotsman that's the name I'd like to be known by. So I am Kirsty to Raymond and everyone else in Scotland and known as Christine down here.

As soon as Alex put my garter on that was the last of the finishing touches and I would soon be ready for the off. The bridesmaids had left and everyone else was gone. It was now just me and my dad and I could hardly believe that this was it; I had waited so long for this moment and at last it was here. I was standing upstairs on the landing when I heard the car arrive. My dad opened the front door and shouted up, "Chris, are you ready?"

I remember feeling so excited as I walked down the stairs and couldn't wait for my dad to see me and tell me how beautiful I looked. We didn't have far to travel as the church was just around the corner. The closer we got to our wedding day it was amazing how many local people already knew about it and would stop us in the streets to wish us well. Many mentioned that they would also be coming down on the day to see us as they wouldn't miss it for the world. I suppose news travels fast in villages and obviously more people knew about us as we would have stood out in the crowd because of our circumstances. We both felt very touched just knowing that so many locals were interested or even cared enough in wanting to come and share in our wedding day, especially when we didn't even know them. I thought if they all kept to their word there would be a huge gathering.

All Saints was quite a large church, with the entrance to the right hand side; there was a lawn at the front and also a driveway to the left which led you up to the church hall and also to a car park around the back. This again give you access to the side entrance of the building. As the wedding car drew nearer to the church the driver commented about the large crowds of people that were gathered and waiting at the front gates. As soon as he said that it put the biggest smile on my face that I felt like a Cheshire cat grinning from ear to ear. It was so uplifting and the most wonderful feeling thinking that so many people had turned out as promised to see us married.

I was that excited and didn't feel nervous at all and I couldn't wait for the wedding car to pull up and to get out and show my wedding dress off but also to soak in all the atmosphere and to listen to all the chit-chat from everyone. This was mine and Raymond's special day and I was determined not to let anyone spoil it for us and also to make sure that we and everyone else enjoyed every minute of it. Within a split second my thoughts and dreams were shattered and my heart sank to the bottom of my feet when the wedding car drove straight up the drive and around the back of the church, away from everyone. I was so shocked and felt like bursting into tears that you could have cut the atmosphere with a knife. Everything happened so quickly with no explanation and although I tried to explain we needed to go back round to the front as everyone was waiting to see us nobody seemed to listen and I was quickly rushed out of the car and into the old side entrance of the church.

As I stood there with my dad who still hadn't uttered a word I felt totally gutted, robbed and sick to the stomach as it wasn't meant to have happened like that. I also couldn't stop thinking about all the people who had turned out to see us as promised just waiting to get a glimpse of me in my wedding dress. They must have also felt robbed and disappointed – goodness knows what was going through their minds and what they thought about it all. I felt I had let them all down. I then realised there was more to this than meets the eye as I felt it in my bones and knew that my mam was behind it all. I didn't want to believe it – *surely she wouldn't stoop as low as this*, I thought, *to deprive me from all the attention and being so happy, especially on my wedding day? Surely not*, but if you knew my mam as well as my dad and I did and had experienced for yourself first-hand the things that she had said, done and carried out then you would begin to understand what I mean and where I am coming from. Yet she could be lovely and as nice as ninepence to me one minute and in a split second change and become this monster and capable of anything the next. She was definitely two different people to me, but no matter what she said I always loved and respected her because of who she was.

My dad and I had to wait a few minutes before we could walk down the aisle. I don't remember why or even if there had been a problem or not but what I do remember is when linking arms with him I could feel the tension in his body growing and then he began to shake. I suppose apart from feeling nervous he would also have seen the disappointment in my face and felt guilty and responsible because of what had happened. I knew it wasn't my dad's fault and that he was only doing what he had been ordered to do by my mam – it was done and there was nothing we could do about it. So I quickly composed myself, put a big smile on my face and said, "right dad this is it, let's go" as I had the rest of the day to look forward to and enjoy.

The proudest moment for me that day was walking down the aisle with my dad and him giving me away. I was so proud to be his daughter and I truly adored him; he was the apple of my eye and I know that I was his as he told me often enough – and now I was more determined than ever not to let my mam spoil or ruin the rest of our day which I knew would make her feel madder than ever.

The whole ceremony in the church was perfect and the page boys were very well behaved considering they were only five and eight years old. George Kirkup was the minister then – what a scream he was, a real bundle of fun, always laughing and telling you funny jokes and stories. He was the only minister I had ever known and heard of who walked around the streets in his full church regalia. You could hear him halfway down the street way before he passed your front door shouting with his loud chirpy voice and hearty laugh. "Good morning everybody," he would say. "Isn't it a beautiful day?" Of course that was when the weather was much better back then. It was amazing how many of the neighbours acknowledged him as he was well loved in the neighbourhood. So you can understand how our service went so well with a minister like that at your side.

Mr Kirkup kept squeezing our hands every now and then – this was the sign he said he would use to let us know that everything was going fine – but when I eventually heard those final words 'I now pronounce you man and wife' it was at long last a dream that had come true for the both of us. By the time we had come out of the church it was hotter than ever; apparently it had been 96 degrees that day. Everything was going fine at first and you know what it's like when you come to have photo-shoots, it all takes time getting everyone together in different groups and positions.

On the day Raymond's mam presented me with a beautiful parasol; she thought of everything. The sun was that hot I could now feel my face beginning to burn so I asked the photographer if it was alright for me to put my parasol up to protect it. He was delighted and thought it would be great to get some photos taken with it up on my own. It obviously took him a few minutes or more to get myself, parasol, wedding dress and veil in the correct position before taking some shots – then all of a sudden my mam appeared and all hell was let loose. Her manner and the foul language she used towards the photographer was totally disgusting and uncalled for; he was only doing his job. I felt more upset and embarrassed for him than I did for me because I was used to it and I knew what she was like. It was all because she felt he was taking far too much time faffing over me and the photos.

He quietly expressed that there was still more to be taken as I had paid for them. She demanded he finished them there and then so we could get on with the reception. "You can take a few more inside and that's it."

She was so cunning and devious and always knew when and how to pick her moments; she waited especially until I was on my own and well away from all the guests knowing that they would all be chatting to one another and not paying too much attention so they wouldn't see or hear the horrible twisted person she really was. It would never have happened to any other member of the family, just me.

She always made me feel like an outcast, the black sheep of the family as if I were an intruder and didn't belong. Yet I never knew why. I was still determined not to let her make me crack up and spoil everything. I was always good at covering up my feelings so that no one would suspect anything was wrong and start asking questions; I would just smile and carry on as normal. I never called my mam to anyone and in saying that I also would never allow others to say anything wrong about her as I didn't want people to think that she was a bad person, and I protected her name for many years.

The rest of the afternoon and the reception went very well and I'm sure everyone enjoyed themselves of course, except my mam. She couldn't help herself by telling me how my wedding day had been one of the worst days of her life and how she had hated every minute of it of which didn't surprise me as I kind of expected to hear something like that. She must have also put the fear of God into the photographer as he had done exactly what my mam had told him to do which sadly left us short of many good photos which should have been taken to put in our wedding album. We had also paid for the wedding car to come back and pick us up after the reception to take us back home but he failed to turn up. No wonder, I wasn't surprised and I don't blame him because he was a one-man band and ran his own business – he wasn't just the photographer he was also the driver and the owner of the wedding car.

We were lucky we didn't have far to go and were more than happy to walk it back. I suppose my mam was laughing up her sleeve and feeling quite proud of herself thinking she had won and ruined our wedding day but instead we were the ones who had the last laugh and came out on top.

I've been saving the best till last to tell you about the little extras that happened on the day. The first being, and unbeknown to us at the time, apparently all the public who had turned out and patiently waited to see my dad and I arrive in the wedding car had felt totally robbed and disappointed about it, so they made sure they weren't going to be left out and all piled into the church to see us getting married. We only had seventy-five guests but I heard the church was full to the brim, holding well over 200 people with the overflow at the back, and apparently there were still many others waiting outside in the grounds which obviously must have set my mum's blood boiling, raging with jealousy. Then at the reception Raymond gave a short speech and presented me with a beautiful half sovereign ring as a wedding present.

But the final and most exciting news was when Oliver Ryder who was our friend and B.P.R.O. stood up and announced that we were going to be the proud new tenants of 89 Cemetery Road in two weeks' time when their daughter and son in law would be moving out. Raymond and I just couldn't believe our luck. We were hugging and kissing each other with excitement and I had tears of joy running down my cheeks; it was a dream come true of which again we thought would never happen to us. That was certainly the icing on the cake for us that day.

Chapter 19

We were going back to Ceres for our honeymoon, to where we first met, which held so many happy and cherished memories for us both (along with a few iffy ones from Alwyn House!). It was a very small, quiet village that would most probably mean very little to anyone else passing through. We were staying at the Meldrums hotel where we went out on our first date together; we were both so excited just thinking about it and just couldn't wait to get there. It was so hard to believe that it was almost four years ago, give or take a day or two, since we were last there; somehow it felt just like yesterday. We caught our train from Newcastle Central Station later that evening after leaving all the family at the Sunniside club to enjoy the rest of the night.

We had to leave then because the only train that was going to Ceres was leaving from Edinburgh the following day. Previously when we travelled backwards and forwards to Edinburgh we always used the coaches from Gallowgate bus station in Newcastle. It may have taken twice as long, or more even, but it was less than half the price the trains were charging which we could simply never afford, so this was a real luxury for us and because it was part of our honeymoon we thought we would go the whole hog and do it in style.

Newcastle Central Station was as dead as a dodo when we arrived and there was certainly no life around from where we were standing. All of a sudden this train pulled in, no one got off and we weren't even one hundred per cent sure if it was ours or not, so we shouted down the platform in case someone else was there but there was no response and we didn't even know where the doors were so we could climb aboard and ask.

We began to panic, not quite knowing what to do next and were sure that the train would be pulling out very shortly without us. Thank goodness that this guardsmen appeared to our rescue; he quickly opened the door, helped us up the steps and put our luggage in the passageway. "Can you manage from here?" he said.

"Yes, no problem," we replied.

What a relief. How lucky we were because as soon as he slammed the door shut the train was ready to pull out. We weren't too sure which direction to go in order to find our right carriage and to be honest it had been a long day and we couldn't be bothered to start trekking all over the place. The guardsmen had placed our luggage to the right side of the carriage so that's the one we decided to go into. When we went to put our cases into the luggage racks they were all empty and there didn't seem to be any other passengers because it was so quiet; that was even better, I thought, as it meant we had the whole carriage to ourselves.

I remarked to Raymond how plush the seat felt as I sat down in it.

"I know what you mean," he said, "I thought the same."

We also had a lovely textured table which we were very surprised at.

"I don't remember anything being as plush as this four years ago, Raymond, when I travelled up to Edinburgh with my mam. Do you think we are in a first class carriage here?" I said.

"I'm not quite sure but it's possible that we could be," he replied.

My little mind began to bobble. I then placed my hand on the window where I felt velvet curtains hanging at either side. I was sure that we were right because I thought second class carriages couldn't have improved this much in such a short period of time. I thought it was great and quite exciting as a matter of fact until Raymond jumped up out of his seat. I asked him where he was going.

"To get the cases," he replied, "and find another carriage before we get into trouble."

I told him to sit back down and we would think it through properly.

I told him that I couldn't be bothered to start faffing about and looking for somewhere else to sit because I was quite happy to stay there as it was lovely and plush and I remarked to him, "when would we ever get the chance to travel first class again – never!"

I explained that we weren't harming anyone or taking anyone else's seat as the carriage was empty but Raymond was worried in case a right grumpy old inspector was to check our tickets and make us move elsewhere. I said to Raymond, "Do you really think for one minute that anyone would ask two people who can't see and have made a genuine mistake to leave an empty carriage whether it's first class or not to sit elsewhere especially when they're going on their honeymoon? I don't think so. Just leave the talking to me."

Sure enough 15 to 20 minutes later in walked the inspector. "Tickets please," he said.

I calmly went into my handbag, pulled them out and handed them to him. He looked at them, paused and then told us that we had second class tickets and that this was a first class carriage we were in. I apologized and explained that because we couldn't see and because there was nobody about to help us when we boarded the train, we just decided to sit here. I mentioned to him that if he wanted us to move it would be no problem. He was a lovely man, maybe in his fifties. He remarked that he was more than sure it would be fine for us to stay there and it wasn't as if we were taking anybody's seats. "Just leave it with me and I'll check it out," he said.

Raymond and I were still holding hands and gave each other a gentle squeeze meaning that we were sure that everything was going to be all right.

He must have only taken a few steps then suddenly stopped and asked, "Are you off on holiday somewhere?"

Raymond and I answered at the same time proudly saying, "We were just married today and are off on our honeymoon."

He was totally overjoyed with our news, shook our hands, congratulated us and gave me a quick peck on the cheek. "Listen here, just you both stay put. I am giving you personal permission myself to travel in this carriage. It's not every day we have honeymoon couples travelling with us so why not do it in style, enjoy it and make the most of it."

As he walked away we giggled and hugged each other tight – once again we couldn't believe our luck and were thrilled to ribbons with the news.

"What did I tell you?" I said. "I just had this feeling and I knew it would all work out."

Within no time the same inspector was back and in jest put on a very posh voice saying, "Sir, Madam, British Rail also offer their congratulations. I would like to offer you both a complimentary drink and sandwich of your choice."

We both burst out laughing and I also replied back in a posh voice, "Madam would like coke and Sir would like whisky, both with salad sandwiches please." It was just getting better and better all the time.

Because we didn't have a great deal of money left we couldn't afford to stay overnight in a hotel in Edinburgh so instead we stayed at Raymond's mum's house and left for Ceres the following morning. We then arrived at the Meldrum's hotel in Ceres just after lunch on the Sunday. Mrs Seath and her family must have seen the taxi arrive and came out to greet us. We were all thrilled to see each other again and there were hugs and kisses all round. What a feeling it was to be back there. Mrs Seath then asked if we would like to come through to the bar for a wee drink before she took us upstairs to our room. She had no sooner opened the door then all of a sudden there was this mighty cheer – the bar was full of well wishers who still remembered us from four years ago. We were totally shocked and didn't expect it. Then this loud voice shouted out "three cheers for the bride and groom". We recognised his voice straight away – it was big Jim White from the Ceres Inn. "Hip hip hooray," they all shouted and clapped. It was awesome, the best feeling ever. It was so strange it made us feel as if we had never been away.

Time was moving on; it was almost two o'clock so we thought we had better go up and unpack, freshen ourselves up then come back down for some lunch. It had been great fun chatting to everyone about days gone by, but before we left and went to our room we thanked them all for the lovely surprise and hoped that we would see them all later. I wasn't prepared for what happened next and didn't quite know what to say when everybody started wolf whistling, cheering and making wise cracks about us leaving to go upstairs to our room so early in the afternoon. I was so embarrassed and could feel my face going bright red at what they were suggesting we were going to get up to. Raymond just laughed but I was so gullible and began to explain that we were only going upstairs to unpack and freshen up, nothing else. Well you can imagine the fun and mick-taking they were having with me; I was just like a piece of putty playing straight into their hands – just as well I had a good sense of humour and laughed it off. Mrs Seath then escorted us to our room; she was also still laughing about what had been said.

Neither of us had ever stayed in a hotel or guesthouse before so it was all very new and exciting for the both of us but even more so because it was our honeymoon.

We knew we were going to have the most fantastic time and was sure that we were going to enjoy every minute of being there. It was quite a large room with a lovely feel to it – apparently it overlooked a large field with two or three horses in it. The room was red hot and you could feel the sun beaming on you through the window.

"Well I'll leave you to it," Mrs Seath said in her lovely soft Scottish voice.

It may have been just a small country pub with a few bedrooms upstairs to others, but to us it was like being at The Ritz and it will always remain our very special little hotel forever. We heard that the Fairleys were still alive and running Alwyn House although they must have been getting on a bit. Not many of the locals had anything good to say about the place or the Fairleys because of the many weird and distressing stories they had heard from some of the trainees who had spent time there.

I tried to prompt Raymond for us to pay them a visit while we were there but he wouldn't hear of it – he was still feeling very bitter at the way we had been treated by them, but as far as I was concerned it was water well under the bridge, something that happened long ago. "We've both moved on since then," I said to Raymond, "and I know it is something that we will never forget but if we don't let it go and put it behind us it means that we are just as bad and as twisted as they are and I will never allow that to happen."

There was this long sigh and pause from Raymond. "Not this time," he said. "I don't want anything to spoil our honeymoon. Maybe some other time in the future."

I was happy with his decision and understood where he was coming from.

We went and visited the other two local pubs we used to go to. We were sorry to hear that Jim had sold the Ceres Inn – as you know it was also a very special place for us but we didn't allow it to spoil our memories. We covered all the walks we once went on and were lucky enough not to get lost this time. We also visited Cupar and reminisced in all the little cafes that we had had so much fun in with all our mad friends from Alwyn House. The weather was terrific and overall we had the most marvellous time, but as they say all good things must come to an end and it was time to leave. We were both so happy that we had chosen to go back there for our honeymoon; it was always something that we had wanted to do and had no regrets, and we now had even more special memories to remember Ceres by.

Chapter 20

We arrived back in Newcastle late Saturday afternoon. It was good to be back, not just to see the family but also to go through all our wedding presents again. You know what it's like on the day, everything is so hectic and there were still many that hadn't been opened yet. So there was another exciting evening ahead of us.

Everyone seemed so pleased to see us back, even my mum was interested to hear all we had got up to and the places we had visited. She sounded really happy for us and was pleased we had a great time. How I wished she was always like this to me because when she was nice she was really nice and we got on well.

One more week and the flat would be ours. We couldn't wait to move in and were counting down the days; I somehow felt that this was the answer to my prayers. I always desperately wanted to believe that there was a God but for many reasons I found it so difficult, but I always tried to keep an open mind. As far as Raymond was concerned he didn't even exist, end of story. Religion and politics was always something I would never argue over because I thought it was always very important to respect other people's views.

Well the holidays are now over and it's back to work. Remember I told you earlier that my B.P.R.O. Oliver Ryder had found me a job a few months ago? What a surprise that was; it came totally out of the blue as I never thought for one minute that I would ever work again. When he told me what type of job it was and also what it entailed it was certainly not what I expected to hear or even thought possible for me to do. The place was called Palatine Products, at Whickham View along Elswick Road in Newcastle. It was a very large, old factory that was purpose built in the early 1900s for the blind so that they had somewhere to go and work. They used to make all different types of cane products to sell such as baskets, trays etc simply because the outside workforce back then most probably thought that this was all the blind were capable of doing; but as time moved on some of the blind were fortunate enough to receive training in typing and telephony which opened doors for them to seek work in the outside industries because by law they now had to employ between one and three per cent of disabled people in their workforce, which was certainly a major step forward and quite rightly so.

When I worked there in 1976, although the name had been changed for a good while to Palatine Products, it was still classed and known by many as the old workshops for the blind. There were two factories; the smaller one was further down the road which was the upholstery department where the blind made three piece suites to the highest standard, and I mean to the highest standard. They were fantastic tradesmen and many of them had worked there for many years. They made lots of different types of suites and designs including the Chesterfield, Queen Anne and so on. They were actually bought and sold from your top high street department stores – that's how good they were. I bet any of the public would be none the wiser about who had made them or where they came from.

The same applied in the part where I worked except that the factory was much bigger where many different types of beds were made. Over the years only blind men had ever been employed and trained as mattress and divan makers as well as those who made the three piece suites, but in April 1976 for the first time ever changes were about to take place. They were now willing to offer a position to a blind female to also be trained as both a mattress and divan maker and only if they were successful this would then open the doors and make way for other blind females to be trained and employed in the same line of work as the men.

I was really excited and couldn't wait to start. It had been almost six years since I worked at Boots the Chemist and this was certainly going to be much different from standing behind the counter and serving the public. I had been told by the management to prepare myself as it was a very skilled, strenuous and mucky job to do. That didn't bother me; I quite liked getting my hands dirty and I was as strong as an ox as I always kept myself fit doing exercises and practising my karate techniques. I was told and understood that I was going to be under strict supervision because everything now lay in my hands to prove whether women were capable of doing the same job here as the men.

What pressure, I thought, *for anyone to have resting on their shoulders.* Well that was it! *Bring it on*, I thought to myself. I was more determined now than ever that I wasn't going to let us girls down and to give the guys a good licking and run for their money – which I did! My hours were 8am till 4pm Monday to Friday. Although I didn't have too far to travel compared to some of the others I still had to leave at 6:30 in the morning if I was to get there in time as I had two buses to catch and if I missed the connections it meant I would be late. Many of the men travelled from all over the borough and had done for many years since they were young boys as this was the only place where they could find work, but there was this one particular guy who had travelled all the way from Alnwick each day for more than 35 years – it was over 40 miles each way and he had to leave the house at five o'clock in the morning if he was to catch his connections and arrive on time. Apparently he had travelled through some of the worst winters on record and had only missed coming to work when the transport was taken off. The same went for many of the others who worked there – now that's what I call total dedication. I think people were made out of something else back then in those days because, if I'm being honest, I don't think I could have done it or even would have wanted to.

It was my first day in the mattress department and they weren't kidding when they said it was a dirty and strenuous job – you were practically your own labourer as well but I was still raring to go and up for the challenge no matter what. All the mattress and divan workers were blind, most of them from birth and a few others from an accident or illness when they were very young so it made me feel quite lucky – at least I had my eyesight until the age of sixteen and I felt I had a big advantage over many of them. I was wondering what type of greeting I would receive from the men – after all, I was the first female to be trained to do a man's job, which would make us equal. How would they feel about that after all these years? But as soon as I was introduced to them they welcomed me with open arms and accepted me straight away as one of the lads which was a great relief. All the machine operators had to be sighted but we did have both sighted and unsighted machinists and it was the same with the office staff. There was also three brothers who worked there; they were all blind, deaf and couldn't speak. One of them was married with four children and one with two children.

Ernie was the upholsterer, the other a joiner and Bob was the tape edger. They were all very highly skilled jobs that they had to do; to be honest myself and many others never knew how they managed to do it but they did and also to a very high standard I was told. It just goes to show that everything is possible and way beyond our understanding. They were obviously three very gifted people and well tuned in by using all their other senses. As the old saying goes where there's a will there's a way and they most certainly proved it. I used to love having a natter with them as they had a wicked sense of humour and liked a good laugh.

A couple of years previously I had attended night classes at the Fountain View for one year learning both the deaf blind and deaf sighted sign language. I thought it was a must that I learnt it as I had many deaf friends at the Fountain View centre and it was important to me that I was able to communicate with them. Apart from that, you never know when it might come in handy and it most certainly did when I worked at Palatine Products.

Chapter 21

The day we had been patiently waiting for had eventually arrived. We were told that we could go over to the agency and pick up the keys to our new flat. Raymond and I were totally elated and couldn't get there quick enough. As soon as we had picked the keys up from Newcastle we immediately jumped on the bus and came straight back over to Gateshead. When we got off and began to walk along Cemetery Road where our flat was the feeling was awesome and we were both on cloud nine and couldn't wait to reach the front door and put the key in the lock.

As we stood side by side Raymond gently pushed the door open. I was just about to take a step forward into the passageway when Raymond stopped me by holding on to my arm. "Wait a minute, Kirsty," he said, "there's something I have to do first." I was just about to ask him what he meant when all of a sudden he swept me off my feet, into his arms and carried me over the threshold down the passageway and into the sitting room on the right before he put me down and said, "Welcome Mrs Deponio to our new home."

I thought it was so romantic and was tickled pink. It was so good to be back here again – the flat had a lovely warm feel to it even though it was empty. It took us only two weeks to get everything done the way we wanted it before moving in with all our furniture. Most of it was second-hand except for our bed, carpets and what Raymond's mam and sister had bought us. Our bedroom furniture, three piece suite, fridge and cooker we bought from my mam when she replaced hers and stored them in a neighbour's spare room and also in my mam's wash house. Everything was just perfect, paid for and we were debt free. Raymond and I thought and felt that everything was beautiful; to a lot of others it may have just been an ordinary two bed flat but to us it was our little mansion and we were King and Queen of the castle.

It was so strange how many different thoughts flashed through my mind the week before we moved into our flat which made me panic a little. It was a big step knowing I was leaving my home, family and my own private bedroom behind. I had lived there for ten years since I was 12 and then all of a sudden it made me realise just how grown up I was and I was no longer that little girl; instead I was now a married woman with responsibilities of my own, but one thing I must say is that my mam taught me well in how to run a home, organize things, handle money and sorting and paying bills which I will always be thankful for and has remained an asset throughout my life.

We were both very happy living at Cemetery Road and the neighbours were all very friendly. Sylvia and Dennis lived up above us with their two sons Tony and Peter. They were a lovely family and nothing was ever a problem if we needed any help of any kind as sometimes we did need a pair of eyes to help us now and then. Also, Sylvia from upstairs, and her sister Joan, who lived two doors down, had also been brought up in the flat which we moved into.

The cemetery was opposite us but had a very high stone wall in front with very tall mature trees and when I stood or sat at the front door the sound from them when they were blowing in the wind was so calming and tranquil. Most of the neighbours on the street were quite elderly and had lived there most of their lives and when the weather was nice we would all gather together outside of Nancy and Dave's house just a few doors along, then out would come the chairs and a couple of small tables with cakes, sandwiches and pots of tea. Everyone was welcome to join them. We used to have a right old laugh with them; they were all very open minded and some of the stories they told you of days gone by were hilarious. That's what I loved about living there – everyone was neighbourly and had time for each other.

Chapter 22

Raymond and I left for work the same time each morning and would catch the bus at the end of the street opposite Bushes the florist at the bottom of old Durham Road. Raymond got off in Gateshead town centre and caught another bus to the Team Valley; I stayed on and travelled to Newcastle and then caught my next bus outside the old Binns department store in Market Street which took me along to Elswick Road and on to Whickham View. I enjoyed going out early in the morning because it was so different, the birds would be whistling, the air was fresher, everything seemed so calm and peaceful, rid of all the hustle and bustle.

One morning I was taken into the manager's office – it was to hear if I was going to be kept on or not. I was thrilled when they told me how happy they were with my work and offered me a full time job; it was good money and I was also on bonus. This meant financially we would be pretty well off with two wages coming in and because we lived in church property our rent was very low. So this meant we had plenty of money spare for our food, bills and also to save up to renew all of our second-hand furniture in the near future to our own taste as well as putting money away for going on holiday to Edinburgh each year to see the family.

At Palatine Products we made all different types of beds and special mattresses such as pocket unit ones and those for ships and hospitals. They also took special orders so that we could make and design any size divan or mattress to fit in all size bedrooms. I loved my job and took real pride in my work in both the mattress and divan department. We all had our own allocated bench to work from and there was also a large pressurised staple gun which hung from above each bench on a special flexi cable for us to do the work with. You were a one man band each making your own product but you also had to be fairly fit and have your wits about you as you were practically your own labourer, dragging and lifting spring-edged frames onto your bench as well as divan bases, but also not forgetting about all the materials that were needed to make them.

The three foot and four foot six cheaper mattress springs were much lighter in weight than the more expensive ones and they came in compressed bundles of ten which were sealed and wrapped in brown paper. They were also bound and held tightly together with thin strips of plastic which were at the top, middle and bottom. It was a real knack opening these roll packs as well as unwinding and rolling the brown paper correctly in order to take each spring out safely one at a time. It didn't matter how careful you were opening them, somehow they seemed to have a mind of their own and could explode by releasing the spring so quickly without any help and would burst through the paper shooting them all over the place. At the time it gave you a fright but afterwards you just laughed about it and felt lucky that you weren't a few fingers short or had a black eye if they hit you in the face.

It was a dirty job as your mattresses were made from fibre, flock and material so you can imagine when it came to turning it over to complete the other side how much rubbish was blowing your way. After a while I was transferred into the divan section where I was trained up to be a divan maker.

I was quite looking forward to working in there. They were all male workers and years older than me; a few of them weren't far off retiring age but they were great guys, very friendly and easy to get along with. I have to say that making divans was definitely for me and I absolutely loved it. I enjoyed making them rather more than the mattresses because there was much more to it. Most of them were folding divans and again you were mainly a one man band responsible for dragging and lifting your own bases on to the bench yourself. For me personally I felt it was more like a work of art as you started from nothing really, just a hollow wooden frame base with bars going across halfway down inside. You then fitted loose cone shaped springs by slotting them through the holes in the metal bars by hand, one at a time, twisting them round and round until they were tight, secure and all bars were full. After that you measured and cut the appropriate amount of strips of webbing that were needed to web all the springs together as well as doing everything else that was needed to be done before finally placing and fitting your material on top. There was a definitely an art and format in fitting the top cover on the divan base as you had to make sure that everything was even and lying in the perfect position with all the folds hanging in the correct place ready for stapling. Some of the covers were edged all the way round with white piping and it was a must, when fitting the cover on, that the piping was always kept in a perfect straight line no matter what, or otherwise your work would not be accepted.

The finishing touches entailed covering and stapling a large hessian dust sheet to the bottom of the divan base before attaching and fitting the metal plates in place that were needed to join and hold the folding divan together, then last but not least banging in all the metal sockets in which to fit the casters in before being bagged and put on the lorry for delivery. For me that was total job satisfaction seeing it through from beginning to end.

I was told that a new blind girl had been employed who would be coming to work alongside me in the divan section which I was looking forward to. Her name was Vivian but she was known as Viv for short. What a character she was; we were about the same age and had roughly been married for the same amount of time. She was 5 foot 8 inches tall, slim build, with black hair page boy style and had a wicked sense of humour. We had a lot of laughs together especially when we played tricks on our foreman Ray McGinty who lost his sight at the age of nine through an accident. He wasn't like what you'd expect a foreman to be – in saying that, not any of them were; they were all a bundle of fun and a joy to work with.

Ray would be about 5 foot 6 inches tall, thick set and a belly like a poison pup – everyone remarked on it and because he liked going out for a drink we called it his little beer pot. Ray would just laugh, pat his stomach give it a good old rub and say, "This is from good food, good living and nothing else." I think he was in his mid-forties and was bald on top with a small amount of hair round the sides and back, a little bit like Friar Tuck from Robin Hood. Viv decided to nickname him Toby Jug because that's exactly what he reminded you of. He loved smoking his pipe and had a great sense of humour, with the most heartiest chuckle and catchy laugh ever. When he laughed you laughed.

Some of the stories he used to tell Viv and me while we were working were hilarious. We never knew whether to believe him or not because he always laughed when he was telling us but he insisted every time he was telling the truth. Some of the tricks that Viv and I played on him though I don't think that anyone else but Ray would have put up with it – that's the type of guy he was. On a very hot day Ray always allowed one of the employees to take an order for ice creams for those who wanted them from the shops. Viv and I always had a choc bar as it was our favourite; we would always save a little ice cream in the bottom of the paper. By this time it would be mushy and runny. One of us would then shout for Ray, pretending we had a problem of some kind with our divan, knowing he would come straight down to help. As soon as he approached the bench we would both pounce on him with our open ice cream papers and because Viv was three inches taller than me, she always took charge of his head while I addressed his face. We both rubbed the ice cream in as fast as we could in both areas. He was such a great sport and most of the time he just stood there without batting an eyelid chuckling to himself while we were laughing our socks off but I suppose because we had played that many different pranks on him over the years he maybe thought to himself why bother struggling, just let them get on with it. He always saw the funny side to everything and laughed with you every step of the way. He was truly one in a million.

Chapter 23

Raymond and I loved being married; we were so happy in our little flat together with nobody breathing down our necks all the time and telling us what to do. It was the most wonderful feeling knowing that we were in charge and could come and go as we please and invite whoever we wanted without asking permission from anyone else.

The only item we never bought when we first got married was a washing machine and it wasn't by choice. My mam had said over and over again that it wasn't necessary for us to have one – we didn't need it as she would do all our washing for us to save us time because of us both working. I don't know how she figured that one out as I kept expressing to her it was no mega deal for me to shove some clothes in the washer and to hang them out to dry, but she wouldn't have it. Instead we actually had to make four journeys a week, two to take them up and another two to bring them back because there were too many clothes for us to carry with all our work gear and towels to do it in one. We both found it very inconvenient as well as time consuming as there were four bus journeys involved each time. Sometimes it could be as late as nine o'clock at night before we got back home which made it a very long day as we had been up from roughly 5:30 in the morning.

At first I really thought that my mam did have our best interests at heart and just wanted to help us out; instead I should've realised that there was a reason behind it all, as always. There was always method in her madness in everything that she said and done. Because we were now married and away from home I was hoping that her behaviour and feelings towards not just me but also Raymond would change somehow for the better but again as the old saying goes a leopard never changes its spots. I don't believe that this is the case for everyone but for some unfortunately it is.

It dawned on me later this was obviously her way of making sure that she was still in control of me. It was as if I was a possession of hers; she was so domineering and demanding throughout my life as if I didn't have a mind of my own or I wasn't allowed to have one and had to be at her beck and call about everything. Things would be fine as long as she got her own way but as soon as I went against any of her decisions all hell would be let loose and my life would not be worth living.

The worst time of all was when I would never give in to her about Raymond having a vasectomy to avoid us having children. No one ever has the right to make such a decision as big as that for you no matter who they are. My mam knew how much it meant to Raymond and me, that's all we ever talked and dreamt about, God willing of course. Her main excuse apparently was always because of hereditary blindness being on both sides of our family and that we could maybe pass it on to our own children. So to avoid any heartache she felt it was best not to go there and to avoid having children altogether. I'm not even saying that she didn't have a valid point – of course she did, but at the same time the decision should have been left with us and she should have honoured that.

I explained many times that as far as I was concerned there were no guarantees in life about anything and what will be will be and if we were lucky enough to have children, disability or no disability we would still love and give them the best start in life that we could ever possibly give. "What about the amount of parents that have both been fit and healthy," I would say, "with no backgrounds of disability or even serious illnesses and yet have still had severely disabled children with no explanation at all?"

I might as well have banged my head off a brick wall and saved my breath as I don't think she ever listened to a word I said or took my feelings into consideration. The final words that she would always finish off with would be, "Look here, just make sure that Raymond gets this vasectomy done as soon as possible and the quicker the better as far as I'm concerned."

I honestly don't know how she could have been so heartless, cruel and as direct as she was expecting us to obey and carry out her ruthless and horrible commands because that's exactly what they were. Anyway we wanted to wait a while before trying for a family so that we could enjoy each other's company, have a few holidays away and also get some money behind us.

Christmas was just around the corner and we were looking forward to spending our first one together on our own. It was obviously going to be very different and much quieter as my mum always had a houseful with all the family being there but we enjoyed it all the same. We went to Edinburgh for the New Year – or Hogmanay as they call it – and had a brilliant time as always.

About every three months I used to invite Raymond's mum to come and stay with us for a month at a time. I just loved having her around; she was no bother and we got on well together. Her favourite shopping place was the indoor market at Gateshead where she spent most of her days while we were at work. At weekends we would take her out to many different places, which we thoroughly enjoyed and had a lot of fun. She also just loved sitting at the front door in the sun watching life go by and having a natter with the neighbours because back home in Edinburgh she lived on the top floor of the tenements. Her feet weren't always at their best as she had a lot of problems with them and didn't go out as often as she would have liked to. It would be enough to put anyone off going out as there were so many stairs to climb up and down each day which I suppose could make you feel quite isolated from everyone. So she certainly made up for it when she came down here to stay with us and who could've blamed her?

Chapter 24

In May 1977 at the age of 23 the doctors finally gave me the
go ahead for my return to the sport that I totally loved and so
desperately missed. I had waited for this moment for seven years
and immediately put the wheels into action, looking to see if there
were any local karate schools in the area as my old one was now
based in Darlington, almost 40 miles away which was too far for us
to travel on a regular basis.

I was thrilled when I managed to find one at the Barley Mow
community centre in Birtley which was only a 20 minute bus ride
away. I was also very lucky that they taught the same style as I was
used to which was wado ryu. Ray Coates was my instructor who
was black belt 2nd dan at the time and a whopping 6 foot 5 inches
tall and he felt it was quite a challenge and was looking forward in
taking me on.

My first time there was the most awesome feeling ever, a dream
come true. There was a good mixture of men, women and children
who were just fabulous. Those seven years seemed to have flown by
so quickly because that night somehow felt as if it was just yesterday
when I had last stood on the dojo floor amongst my fellow karate
men and I was that excited I couldn't wait to start and get into action.

Ray remarked how impressed he was with my performance
that night considering how long I had been away from the sport,
so it just goes to show that all the training I had put in over the
years at home had certainly paid off. There was still much more
that I needed to learn as well as a huge amount of hard work and
dedication to put in if I were to achieve my next two brown belts but
most of all, my ultimate goal in being able to reach my black belt 1st
dan.

Although it was an awesome feeling being back in training in a large dojo hall it was also a little scary – not that I would admit it at the time though. With not being able to see it made everything sound so loud and echoey and when we were all on the floor training at the same time it made me feel quite disorientated, but like everything else through time you adapt and get used to it. The only difference in learning and doing karate back then was that I needed to listen more carefully, concentrate harder and also to pay attention to the vibrations in the floor through my feet, especially when I was free fighting my opponent.

We covered most of our basic training techniques every session for approximately one hour before moving on to anything else. This was very important not just to build up our stamina but also to help us to perform and develop better techniques and stances. My favourite part was learning and performing katas which is a total art on its own. There are many different individual named katas which are put together with a sequence of different karate moves and my favourite ones were Chinto and another called Ku Shan Ku which was the longest kata of all with 72 movements in. The higher the grades the more difficult everything became as the pass rates were very high and nothing was handed out willy-nilly. If you wanted to reach the top and get there you really had to train hard and work your butt off.

By the end of May 1978 I had accomplished both of my brown belts and was now preparing for the karate championships which our school had entered, held in Chester near the border of North Wales. There were 1200 entries from all around the country and about 15 to 20 judges altogether, some of them reaching grades as high as 6th and 7th dan. Some of the judges were Japanese and had even travelled all the way from Japan to be there. It was an all day event and the final was to take place in the evening which made it a very long day for those who qualified and got through. A few had entered from our school. It was quite nerve-racking but a challenge and a marvellous experience.

The venue was huge and the main hall was massive; there were also other rooms elsewhere so you certainly had to be alert and have your wits about you and make sure that you covered all your registrations in the correct areas as well as making sure you didn't miss out on any of your call ups for your competitions, because if you missed out on one you were disqualified from them all as they were very strict. The day was hectic, noisy and buzzing with so much atmosphere as there were many competitions taking place every minute throughout the entire day.

Both men and women of the same grades competed against each other in the kata competition. Approximately 15 at a time would be called up on to the floor. We were told that we would all have to perform the same kata at the same time. If you didn't know them inside out or off by heart you didn't stand a chance, simply because not any of us knew what kata we had to do until we were all on the floor in our stances ready and waiting to begin. Only three to four of the best were chosen from each round in order to enter for the next one. There were quite a few rounds to get through before reaching the semi-finals which got tougher and tougher along the way.

By the end of the day I had actually qualified and got through all my heats and had reached the finals that were to be held later on that night. I was totally elated but also gobsmacked as I was apparently the only one from our school who managed to get through which was also hard to digest. At the time I didn't realise just how big an event this karate championship was.

The final was to be held in the huge main hall. We were given a three hour break, long enough for us to have something to eat and to practise our chosen kata for the final. They also needed the time to set the scene both upstairs and downstairs for the spectators. As the hall began to fill it seemed to become hotter than ever and I began to get a headache. I was terrified in case it turned into a full blown migraine as I suffered badly from them and I knew if it did I wouldn't be able to function as I can become quite ill, so I lay down on the floor and put my bag underneath my head and tried to switch off and relax by rubbing my forehead. *Of all times,* I thought, *for this to happen, typical.* I began to feel sick and my body was beginning to tremble slightly, then my breathing started to change. I panicked and had to sit up, then I realised that it wasn't just my head making me feel like that, it was also the thought of me going out to perform on my own in such a big arena in front of hundreds of people.

There was no doubt about it, how worried and anxious I had been feeling, I was literally scared out of my wits with fear. I think it was also because I was still in shock and unprepared really as I never thought for one minute that I'd ever even get through the first round never mind reaching the finals. If I was to succeed that night in anything at all, it was important for me to hurry up and get myself pulled together as time was ticking away. I needed to get my body in tune and mind focussed and also to practise my kata because that's what everybody else seemed to be doing.

This was probably one of the biggest moments and challenges of my life and maybe the only chance ever to prove what I was capable of doing in my karate career. I didn't want to blow it and let my school and my instructor Ray down, but most of all myself. It was also important to me to show others that no matter what disability any of us have, with dedication and determination anything and everything is possible. Again as the old saying goes, where there's a will there's a way! There were no allowances ever made because of me being blind and I wouldn't have wanted it any other way.

Sandra Coates, who was Ray's wife, was also a black belt and she was a lovely person who looked after me and helped to keep me calm. I had heard that the standards were extremely high but I could only do my best and nothing else. I don't think anyone realised just how much more difficult it was for me than those who could see especially when it came to doing katas more than anything else. It was because every movement, posture and stance I did had to be perfect otherwise I couldn't carry on as I'd be going in the wrong direction completely which I had done many times before and would be disqualified. The hardest part was when I had to keep my stance and position correct when having to pivot right round quickly on one foot from one direction to the total opposite and then do a flying kick in the air and land down in the perfect stance, position and straight line. At first, like everything else, you think you will never conquer it and get there, but when you keep training and practising your movements over and over again it's amazing how your brain just takes over, kicks in and adapts to it somehow. Everything just seems to fall into place and becomes like second nature to you.

The finals started off with the three fighting competitions at first which was very exciting. The Japanese judges may have been very loud, abrupt and strict but nobody got away with anything from them, which in every aspect I feel was a good thing because it meant what anybody achieved that night they won it fair and square.

After the free fighting competition the finals of the kata championship began. It seemed to go on for ages as there were quite a few finalists to get through before the final presentation. There were only three trophies to be given out, 1st 2nd and 3rd place. Sandra was keeping me informed about everybody's performance as the standards were so high and I was also competing against dan grade students who were much higher than myself. It was anyone's game really. All I knew was that I had to give the performance of my life – which I did. I was practically one of the last ones to perform and unfortunately I made a slight error at the very end of my kata by turning in the wrong direction, so instead of facing the judges I ended up with my back to them. Apparently I was lying in second place until that point and was then dropped to fourth place and out of the trophy position altogether. It was no good crying over it; it was done and that was that! Unfortunately that's the way the cookie crumbles sometimes. When it came to the presentation time all of us competitors were sitting on the floor waiting patiently to hear who had won. I would be lying if I said that I wasn't a little disappointed in missing out on receiving a trophy. Especially when I had almost been in hands' reach of it.

When the championships had almost come to a close one of the judges made an announcement and said that there was still one more very special, important trophy that was to be given out. It was the Stella Williams trophy for outstanding achievement in karate which was apparently the highest award to be given out on the day and to only one individual person who they felt had outshone everyone else and performed to the highest standard throughout the entire day and night. When I heard them shout out my name I was speechless and almost in tears. I truly never expected it to be me. The atmosphere was both awesome and breathtaking and when I went out to receive my trophy I was told that the whole arena was up on its feet giving me a standing ovation. Everyone was cheering and clapping so loudly that I couldn't even hear what the judge was saying to me and got a shock when he put the trophy in my hands. It was huge and must have weighed quite a bit. I was so happy and thrilled to have received it and couldn't wait to get back home and tell Raymond the good news.

As we travelled back that night on the bus I was still finding it very hard to digest and couldn't get my head around it all. It was the fact that out of 1200 competitors the award was given to me which was a very humbling experience and one which I will never forget.

It was amazing how the news travelled so fast. The day after I arrived back from Chester I had both the press and TV on the phone wanting to come and interview me about my achievement. Over a short period of time I appeared in quite a few local newspapers telling my life story as well as appearing on good old

Look North, Today at Six and also Nationwide.

All of a sudden one day out of the blue, I was invited to go down and appear on one of my favourite programmes at the time which some of you may remember called Pebble Mill at One. Bob Langley was the main host of the show then and was also from the North East. I remember him telling me when he heard I was coming down to be on the show that he asked his manager specifically if he could do the interview with me because we were roughly from the same neck of the woods. Well, after all, us Geordies have to stick together. He was a lovely man, a real gentleman to be precise. I also met Hinge and Brackett who were quite big celebrities back then but they were definitely not my cup of tea. It was the first time I had ever performed karate on TV which I have to say was quite nerve-racking, more so as it was going out live. There was certainly no room for any mistakes which I am pleased to say I managed not to make. Thank goodness!

Lee, 7 months old

Lee's Christening – Gloria holding the baby and Raymond's mam on the right

Lee aged 18 months

Blind Athletics UK Championships

Gateshead Blind Athletes

Me with the Stella Williams trophy, 1978
(For outstanding achievements in karate)

In 1979 I was presented with the Wilkinson Sword and Silver Salver.

I was the first recipient and the only woman to be awarded the Wilkinson Sword. I was also the only person ever to be awarded a Silver Salver, for being the world's first blind female black belt in karate.

On holiday in the Isle of Man, with Frank Carson (left) and Cilla Black (right)

Christine tackles her biggest challenge

CHRISTINE Deponio used her karate black belt to full advantage yesterday.

The 28-year-old housewife scored three spectacular tries against an all-male opposition in a friendly rugby match.

It was a remarkable debut for Christine, but what made it all the more special was that she, and the other nine players, were all blind.

Christine, of Cemetery Road, Gateshead, joined her husband Raymond to take part in what is thought to have been Britain's first-ever rugby match for the blind.

Loudspeakers, blaring out pop music at one end and Dr Who stories at the other, guided the two teams as they carried a specially adapted ball about the Gateshead Fell ground.

Dr Who certainly seemed to be a more attractive target for the players, with 18 of the 24 tries scored during the game landing at his end.

The ball, donated by a visiting team of blind Norwegians last year, was fitted with an electronic bleeper to help the players as they charged about the pitch.

Christine, who is also an enthusiastic athlete, took one nasty tumble after a heavy tackle during the 30-minute game, but said she was keen to carry on with the sport.

"I didn't think they would let me play, but I came along anyway and I'm glad I did," she said.

Christine on the attack

Making the news – the only woman to play in the all-blind rugby match

Chapter 25

Once again Christmas was just around the corner and we were both looking forward to a break. Since I had come back from the Chester karate championships in May I had been working extra hard, training three times a week, as I was preparing for my first dan grade for that coming January in 1979. There was so much that I had to learn during the six months, one part being the three new advanced katas. There were some very tricky and complicated moves in them, which I thought I would never conquer, as they seemed so impossible for me to do. Just as well Ray and Sandra Coates believed in me and also gave me all the help and support that I needed in order to help me reach my goal. I managed to keep up and do most things in class with other students by verbal instruction because of my past experience in karate from when I could see.

The only main problem I ever had was when learning something new which was totally impossible under the circumstances for me to fully understand from verbal instruction only, so therefore I had to learn all the other movements and stances by touch. My instructors between them must have spent dozens of hours teaching me on a one-to-one basis, patiently taking me through step-by-step every single movement, time and time again. Together, with the encouragement and faithful support of Ray and Sandra Coates and also my wonderful husband Raymond who came along each week and sat through every session, this all helped me to finally fulfil my ultimate goal and dream to receive my black belt in 1st dan. Thank you.

So again it just goes to show through hard work, dedication and faith that any of us can achieve our most ultimate goals and dreams, no matter how big or small they may be. It doesn't matter whether we are able bodied or severely disabled – I believe that there is hope for everyone as I am living proof of that. If I can do it then anybody can.

Chapter 26

In February 1979 just a few weeks after getting my black belt Raymond and I, and also my instructor Ray and his wife Sandra, were invited to attend the Newcastle sports council dinner, to be held on Tuesday the 13th of March at Newcastle Civic Centre for the Newcastle sports personality awards. Raymond and I were thrilled at the thought of being invited to such an occasion and I couldn't help but wonder why. It was formal dress so I was looking quite forward to going out and buying a new outfit. I remembered the building very well from the time when I could see – it was absolutely magnificent and at night it was lit up with purple floodlights which made it look spectacular. I've also heard that it still looks just as good today as it did back then. It was officially opened on the 14th of November 1968 by King Olav V of Norway and was mainly designed by George Kenyon along with some other architects, but George was the main city architect for Newcastle at the time and his work is known all over the world especially in Canada. I'm not surprised to hear that he has won so many awards for his outstanding work worldwide. I would also like to add and say that I feel he has certainly done us all proud here in Newcastle.

The first time I had ever set foot in the building was on the evening of the awards and what a night it was. The men had their tuxedos on and Sandra and I wore a long evening dress. I never thought that getting out of a taxi could be so exciting as the place was buzzing with so many people arriving from all directions. There were cars pulling in and out, one after the other, and the atmosphere was fantastic – and that was before we got inside the building. Sandra was just great; she always made sure that we never missed out on anything and described the whole foyer to us and

kept us informed about everything that was happening. It was
unbelievable how big the place was, the foyer must have held at
least a couple hundred or more and there was also this magnificent,
huge, open planned, curved staircase which led to a large landing
at the top. There were also enormous hanging chandeliers. It was
just like being in The Glenn Miller Story where everyone gathered
down below in the entrance hall waiting for the big band to begin
playing at the top. There were so many big sporting stars there like
Brendan Foster, Brian Clough and Jackie Charlton. I was totally
dumbfounded and wondered what the heck I was doing there as
most of them were big VIPs and I was just plain little me, a no one
really.

The meal was spectacular and there were 600 guests there. I had
never experienced anything like it, having never been invited to
such an important and grand affair like that before. Although I was
enjoying myself and also felt so privileged to have been invited, I
still couldn't help but feel a little uncomfortable and out of place as
if someone ordinary like me shouldn't have been there. When the
award ceremony began it was difficult at first to understand all that
was said as the PA system wasn't at its best, but as the night went
on it improved. When I heard what some of the sporting stars had
done to achieve their awards I was just amazed – it then made me
feel more confused than ever as to why I had been invited. Nothing
seemed to make any sense at all.

They then introduced the last award of the evening which was
the Wilkinson Sword award. Apparently it was the first of its kind
ever to be given out which obviously made it extra special for the
person who was to receive it. It was to be presented to someone
whom they felt was a sporting star and for their outstanding
achievement in sport. When the spokesperson began to speak
and tell the story about this person whom they felt was such an
inspiration to others and about the battles that they had faced to
get through to become this sporting star today, I didn't have a clue

who they were talking about – and to be honest I never gave it much thought as I knew very little background about some of the sporting stars back then. It could have been anyone as they gave nothing away, no names were ever mentioned. I suppose there were many others there that night who thought exactly the same as I did: who could it be?

It seemed as if they had gone on for ages talking about this person – well that's what it certainly felt like at the time. I suppose it was because after the opening speech I couldn't understand everything they were saying which was pretty frustrating, only being able to catch bits of words here and there. Again I wasn't too sure if it was the PA system playing up or maybe it had something to do with where we were sitting as we were quite a distance from the speaker and the presentation area. It definitely made me lose my concentration and my mind had drifted off on to other things, even though I knew it shouldn't have.

Then I remember hearing clapping in the background and thought I had heard my name mentioned but to be honest I wasn't too sure as I was miles away. I nearly died when Sandra nudged me and said, "It's you that they're talking about. You need to get up and go out."

I had never felt so embarrassed and stupid in all my life as I still sat there. I could feel my face going bright red as I was totally shocked; somehow it didn't seem real and I found it difficult to absorb. I eventually stood up and went out to collect my award. I could feel myself shaking and actually thought I was walking in slow motion. Everyone was still clapping and cheering as I was guided through the crowds to the front. When they put the award into my hands I got the shock of my life; with not being able to see, I didn't think for one minute that it was going to be an actual real full-length Wilkinson sword mounted on to a large wooden plaque. It was about four feet long and quite heavy to hold.

As I walked back to my seat it was the most wonderful feeling

ever as everyone clapped and cheered me once again on the way.
They made me look as if I were a hero and a big star of some kind,
which I wasn't – I was just plain little me and no one else. As soon
as I arrived back at my seat I was so taken aback when some of the
guests came over to congratulate me and ask me for my autograph.
I remember laughing and asked if they were having me on but they
were deadly serious. So, there I was signing autographs, some were
personal for themselves and others were for their children as they
saw me as their hero and idol and had collected all the newspaper
cuttings which I was in and apparently they loved it when they saw
me on TV.

The biggest shock of all was when Brian Clough came over and
introduced himself to me. He also asked for my autograph and
said that he was one of my biggest fans. I couldn't help but laugh
and asked if he was joking, but he also remarked how serious he
was and meant every word he had said. He was a real lovely man
and we had a very nice chat with each other. I honestly never in my
wildest dreams thought for one minute that I actually had fans and
followers out there.

Many people seemed to leave the main function hall once the
awards were over and gathered together in the foyer where they
still nattered and drank. Raymond was just chuffed to ribbons
and kept saying how proud he was of me. I was still on a high and
couldn't quite believe that I had been nominated for such an award
and especially being the first person to ever receive it. Although I
felt very honoured and privileged then, and still do today, I have
often taken myself back over the years to that night and have asked
myself the same question over and over again: how and why was
I ever chosen that night? Over the last 34 years since 1979 the
Wilkinson Sword has been awarded to a different nominee each
year and today I am still the only woman who has ever received it.
I was also presented with a Silver Salver that night and apparently
I am the only person who has ever been awarded one – this was in

recognition of being the first blind female black belt in karate in the world.

Chapter 27

Each year we went up to Edinburgh for our holidays which we always enjoyed, but in 1980 for the first time we thought we'd have a change and decided to go over to the Isle of Man instead. We were told by many what a beautiful place it was and that there were many places to visit, lots to do and that it was also a very small island, which suited us both down to the ground. It meant that we felt safer and wouldn't get lost so easily.

It was a lovely journey both there and back and we stayed in quite a large guesthouse which was huge compared to the Meldrums Hotel. We went for two weeks and were going to make sure that we enjoyed every minute of it and missed out on nothing. The weather couldn't have been better as it was red hot every day. There was a real good mix of lovely people who stayed at the guesthouse. It was mainly known as the Irish and Glaswegian fortnight and most of the guesthouses were full of them so you can imagine what fun we had together. They were all real good sports, both young and old. We managed to visit most places and enjoyed a ride on the trams.

The highlight for me was when we went to this huge nightclub that had been recommended to us. When we went inside it was heaving with so many people – they weren't kidding when they said it was big: it must have held well over a thousand or more. There wasn't a pick of bother; everyone just seemed to be having a great time – I know we were. A couple from our hotel told us to go there because of the fantastic entertainment and cabaret. When we paid to get in we never thought to ask what was on and hoped we were in for a surprise.

Fiddly Gig was the first act and they were fantastic singers and comedians and apparently travelled all around the country performing their act. The highlight for us though that night was when Frank Carson came on; what a surprise that was. We didn't realise that they would have big stars like that there and he was brilliant as usual. I always loved him on TV and he was a very humble and friendly man when we met him. We were standing at the very back of the room near the bar as we were unable to get a seat anywhere. When Frank finished on stage he came over to get a drink and was just standing a few feet away from us.

He had everybody laughing at the bar. I had my camera with me so I asked if we could have a photo taken with him. He was so ordinary, no airs and graces, and was happy enough to do it. Then he insisted on buying a drink for us and even stayed and had a chat – how many of your big stars would have taken the time to do something like that? He was a real joy to be with.

We then heard that Cilla Black was coming the following week; she was one of my biggest idols and had been for years. The show couldn't come around quick enough and when it did you could have blown me away as she was just marvellous, out of this world as a matter of fact. It was the best ending to the most fabulous holiday ever.

When she finished I made enquiries to see if it was possible for us to have a photo taken with her. We didn't hold out much hope though as we were told she had already gone back stage but I wasn't prepared to just leave it at that. I explained how she had been my idol for years and would have just loved to have met her for a couple of minutes – well you don't get anywhere if you don't ask. I couldn't believe it when he came back and said she'd agreed to see us. My heart was beating faster than ever when we went back stage to meet her – what a feeling it was when I actually stood beside her in the flesh; there was no airs and graces with her either. The guy had already told her our names so straight away in her Liverpool accent she said, "Hello Christine, hello Raymond, lovely to meet you," and gave us both a big hug. "Did you enjoy the show?"

"Brilliant!" I said. There were so many things that I wanted to ask her but I knew I couldn't as there wasn't time. She then took our hands and rearranged us, stood in between and put her arms round our shoulders. "Right kids," she said, "big smiles and say cheese."

She was just everything I expected her to be and more; I was just in heaven and I'd had the best night ever. We've never been back to the Isle of Man since then but you never know: one day we might just go back and pay the place a visit.

Chapter 28

The first week of January in 1981 I went down like a ton of bricks with a real severe bout of flu, the worst I'd ever had, and I actually took to my bed for almost three weeks. If I wasn't freezing cold and shaking I would be sweating bucketfuls. I was that ill I could hardly lift my head off the pillow and felt as if somebody had beaten me up all over my body. Raymond was always a right little nurse when I wasn't well but this time I could tell he was more worried than ever and called the doctor out. He wasn't the only one who was worried – so was I and I tried not to let it show.

The doctor told him the usual, plenty of fluids, keep her warm and give her some paracetamol when needed. So that was it: against my will he went out and bought an electric over blanket. He knew how terrified I was of using one as I had heard so many frightening and disturbing stories about them but this time I didn't have a say in the matter as I was too ill and weak to argue. I remember that day so well as if it were yesterday – he charged into the bedroom like a bull in a china shop clumping around with his cowboy boots on and began to pull the blankets off the bed just leaving the sheet on. I wanted to tell him to pack it in whatever he was doing as I felt so cold and like a rag doll with no energy and couldn't be bothered with all the fuss. *Thank goodness*, I thought, when he put the blanket back on the bed because by then I wasn't just cold, I was freezing and shaking from head to toe. All of a sudden this beautiful warm feeling began to spread right across my body and I could feel myself beginning to relax and I wasn't shaking as violently as I had been.

I managed to force myself to speak and what a struggle it was; all I wanted to do was just go to sleep. "What's happening, Raymond?" I said. "What's happening?"

He quickly replied, "It's an over blanket, Kirsty. You need it badly and you're using it whether you like it or not and it's not going back to the shop, end of story."

Well that was me told good and proper. I thank God that Raymond took it upon himself that day to go and buy that over blanket because there were times when I felt so ill that I really thought I wasn't going to make it. It was a total life saver, not just for me but also for the baby I felt I was carrying and I was terrified in case I lost it. I was so pleased when I began to feel much better and more like myself and hoped I'd never be in such a position like that ever again with the flu as it had been a very scary experience.

We had been trying for a family for over eighteen months but I was more than sure I was pregnant as I had missed a period and I was always on time. I was getting really excited and found it difficult keeping it from Raymond. I wanted to tell him but I thought it was best just to wait a little longer in case I was wrong because I knew how upset and disappointed he would have been.

Raymond returned back to work the last week in January after looking after me. On two occasions that same week when he came home from work he no sooner walked through the door and asked if I had any chocolate anywhere. When I said no, what a state he went into. He went looking in the fridge, raking through the cupboards and was gutted when he found nothing as he actually needed it there and then. I've never seen him like that before over a bar of chocolate – he could usually take it or leave it.

I started laughing because I thought it was hilarious and couldn't stop. Raymond didn't quite see it the same way but apparently he'd been like that all day and had gone round all the lads in the factory asking them for some but nobody had any. He then remarked how they all laughed at him and said, "Hey your lass isn't pregnant, is she?" I nearly died when he blurted it out. "Are you? Do you think you could be pregnant, Kirsty, and that I'm having a fancy here?"

I felt really bad when I said no to him – he was so disheartened and that desperate that he went straight back out into the pouring rain to get a bar from the garage along the road. That then confirmed what I already felt and thought more than ever. The following day I decided to phone the doctors' surgery up and explained my situation to them. They then gave me an appointment for my first check-up and examination. It was then when I decided to tell Raymond as I couldn't keep it to myself any longer as I now knew without a shadow of doubt that I was. The morning we went up to the doctors' to have my first check-up done was quite exciting, but at the same time I still couldn't help but feel a little nervous in thinking what would I do if I was wrong! Even though I had put some weight on and some of my clothes were becoming tight it was strange how still in the back of my mind I couldn't relax until I heard it from them.

At the end of the examination we were finally given the news and when we heard those words 'you are definitely having a baby' we were just totally cock-a-hoop and practically crying with joy.

It was the most wonderful feeling ever, knowing that we were going to be parents. We had dreamt of this moment for so long and it was now here. We couldn't wait to get back home to phone everyone and tell them the good news. The only person who concerned me the most was my mam because I didn't know what her reaction would be like when we told her. This was because she had been so bitter and twisted for that many years telling us not to have children and would never stop bullying us about it as well as everything else. For the four and a half years we had been married there were times when I was ill because of it. She also blamed Raymond and held it against him for not doing something about it to prevent it from happening.

The following night we went straight up to my mam and dad's house from work to tell them the news. We thought it was only right to do it face to face and not on the phone. Somehow I felt very calm that night and couldn't wait to tell them both. I knew that my dad would be thrilled but still wasn't too sure about my mam and just hoped that she would be happy for us. As we walked down the street to their house we both felt as proud as punch and were laughing and giggling like a couple of school kids.

A couple of neighbours passed us in the street and said hello. We felt as if we wanted to tell everyone our news. I suppose anybody passing us that night maybe thought we were drunk and how right they would have been – not with booze though, but with joy! That's the only way I can explain it. When we arrived we went straight into the living room. We had decided before we went in we wouldn't beat around the bush and get straight to the point as the tension and excitement was killing us. We stood in the middle of the room with our arms around each other's waist. I started to speak with a big cheesy grin on my face which I couldn't seem to switch off.

"We've got something to tell you," I said. I was just about to tell them both but as quick as a flash my mam jumped in and took me by surprise by saying, "You're pregnant, aren't you?" She then followed by saying, "Your face said it all, as soon as you walked in the room I knew."

My dad came straight over and gave me a big hug and congratulated us. I could tell how pleased he was. My mam on the other hand played it very low key but overall it was very pleasant and everything went well. All I wanted now was for my mam to be pleased for us and to allow me to enjoy my pregnancy.

Chapter 29

A couple of years previously, in 1979, when I knew we were going to try for a family I had decided to put in for a guide dog. I felt having a baby was a very big responsibility and obviously it would be totally dependent on me so I thought that this would be the safest and best option of all in helping to prevent both myself and my baby from any harm or accidents that might occur otherwise.

I was told at the time when I applied that it could take quite a while to get a guide dog simply because they have to make sure that the dog they choose is the perfect match in every way for the trainee, meaning their height, build, age, personality and also in case there are any special needs. I hadn't heard anything from the guide dog centre for quite a while so as soon as it was confirmed that I was expecting I got in touch with them straight away to explain my circumstances to them. I was hoping that they would be able to hurry things along and hopefully find me a suitable guide dog in time and well before the baby was due, as this was the main reason why I had put in for one.

A couple of days later I received a telephone call from Dave Duncan, the manager of the Forfar guide dogs centre. Apparently the doctors at the other end had expressed grave concerns about me getting a guide dog especially with me being an epileptic and thought it would be best for me to be taken off the list as they weren't happy about it. I certainly let my feelings be known and told Dave Duncan how disgusted I was with their decision and felt that I was being victimized because of my illness, through no fault of my own. I also wanted some answers, mainly to know why it had taken them so long to make such an important decision like that after having my medical records for over two years and they hadn't uttered a word before now. Dave really took on board my feelings about what I had said and understood where I was coming from.

He apologized on behalf of the doctors and remarked how upset and taken aback he was himself about the decision that had been made and thought it could have been handled in a far better and compassionate way than it had.

He explained and said unfortunately that the decision didn't lie with him as it was the doctors who would have the final say. He did promise that he would put my case forward to them once more but couldn't promise anything. That's all I wanted: one more chance to be heard and I knew whatever decision was made afterwards that I would have to accept it no matter how strongly I disagreed or not.

So you can imagine how I felt when I received the phone call from Dave with the good news that the doctors had given me the OK to go up. I was totally thrilled and couldn't wait to go out and buy all the necessary clothing and waterproofs from the list they sent me so that at short notice I would be prepared. Four weeks later I received a phone call from Dave Duncan to tell me they had managed to find me a compatible guide dog and asked if it would be possible for me to travel up to Forfar in a week's time. The only downside of my going away was that I wouldn't see Raymond for a month as that was how long the course took. We had never spent a day apart in the eight years he had been down here so it was going to be tough for the both of us.

I travelled up on the Friday and was met at the other end by one of the trainers and taken to the centre by a minibus. It was quite a large place and we had a few people there that were already halfway through their training course. Everyone was very friendly and made me feel welcome. The week entailed lectures and film shows teaching you all the dos and don'ts about guide dogs and their training along with a guided tour of both the inside and outside of the building. I briefly met Dave Duncan before he left to go and spend a week with his young child who was critically ill with terminal cancer.

All the trainees had their own private room with a large empty dog basket in it waiting to be filled with their own personal guide dog. I was so excited and could hardly wait until the Sunday afternoon to meet mine. His name was Sabin and he was quite a large dog with the most beautiful wavy coat. He was a cross between a Golden Labrador and a Retriever and from the first moment I met him we connected immediately. I found it a very moving experience and actually had a big lump in my throat and fell in love with him straight away. It was because he wasn't just this ordinary dog; he had been specially trained and was carefully chosen and given to help me.

My first week of training with Sabin went brilliantly. There was a lot of hard work involved and to be honest I didn't realise that there was so much to learn but together we made a great team and when I was out working with him on the main streets I had complete trust in him and felt totally safe in his hands which was so important for both of us really. I was looking forward to hearing what was in store for our second week of training but unfortunately I took ill with diarrhoea and sickness along with some of the other trainees. I was still taking medication for my epilepsy but because of the diarrhoea and sickness my tablets had obviously flushed straight through my system which caused me to take a slight seizure.

The manager who was left in charge for that week called in the local doctor who was involved with the centre. After checking me over he told me to relax for a few hours and he would come back later to see how I was. My trainer then came in and took Sabin away as he needed to be fed and watered. I was very upset and expressed how worried I was in case the doctor decided to take Sabin away from me because of what had happened.

"Don't you worry about a thing," he said. "Nothing like that would ever be allowed to happen here" – but believe you me it did and that was the last time I ever saw Sabin again. The doctor didn't just leave me gutted; he left me totally broken hearted! The whole centre was up in arms with disbelief and all the trainers were furious and raging about it. The only two who didn't give a toss, flicker or budge an inch were the manager and the doctor. They were definitely two of a kind; they were both near retiring age and horrible nasty people who thought they were far more superior and way above everyone else and I wasn't the only person who thought that – there were many others who did as well.

One of my trainers was about six foot four and built like a tank. He was furious when he heard that the doctor and manager had already arranged another blind woman to come the following day to start her training with Sabin especially without discussing it with him or anyone else. He was that mad he actually punched the bedroom wall so hard with frustration and badly injured his hand.

The doctor and manager continued to blabber on and on, trying to justify themselves to me about what they had done and why, which made me more upset by the minute. They were so cruel and heartless and couldn't understand what all the upset and fuss was about as it was only a dog to them and apparently they had done all of this with my best interests at heart, because of me expecting a baby. Well that was it! They had really overstepped their mark, there was no more Mrs nice guy sitting back and taking any more crap like that from them. They may have been twice my age and had a high position but that didn't give them the right to talk down to me as if I was stupid, a nobody and a second class citizen. There was no way I was allowing anyone to use my baby as a scapegoat to help make them feel better because of their bad behaviour, selfish and uncaring ways – no way! I certainly gave them a piece of my mind about what I thought about them, their rules and Forfar.

From that day many changes were made at Forfar especially to their rules and regulations which excluded pregnant women and epileptics from guide dog training. For the life of me I have never yet been able to understand how a doctor could have and was allowed to make such a final decision regarding who could and could not receive guide dog training. I felt it was a massive slap in the face against people's human rights that should never have been allowed to happen. It may have just been a dog to him as he said, but Sabin was much more than that to me. He became my eyes, which that doctor robbed me of by taking him away. I also said to the doctor that I hoped he would never be in the same position as me one day, because only then he would be able to understand how I really felt and realised just what a terrible thing it was that he had done.

Chapter 30

I had the most marvellous pregnancy and have to say that I just
loved being pregnant. I felt very lucky not to have suffered with any
sickness, likes or dislikes which I suppose all added to it. I found it
fascinating just knowing that this little human being, who was mine
and Raymond's baby, was growing inside of me. We would both be
so excited when the baby moved in my stomach and we'd quickly
place our hands on top trying to see if we could feel a little foot,
arm or anything really. It was exciting times and we were very much
looking forward to becoming proud parents.

I had always said that if we had any children and I was working
that I would give up my job so that I could spend all the time in the
world with them and bring them up as I didn't want to miss out on
anything. So I worked right up until seven weeks before the baby
was due so that I would be eligible to claim all that I was entitled to.
I was sorry to leave Palatine Products because I had really enjoyed
the five and a half years I'd worked there. Apart from that I had
also met and worked with a lot of lovely people. Working there also
helped me to mature and grow up, but most of all it had given me
greater confidence and had helped tremendously towards making
me more mobile and independent which put me in good stead for
coping and managing a family.

There had been one good thing that came from my being at
Forfar and that was meeting Sheila Tyrell who was also blind.
She was a terrific person and I learned so many good tips from
her as she was also married and had a young son. Somehow she
always seemed to have all the answers to my worries and problems
especially the main one of how to manage using my pram and
pushchair safely. "Easy," she said. "You just simply pull it behind you

like a trolley shopper." That's exactly what she'd done and managed perfectly. Through life I feel we learn so much from others as well as from everything we have done and covered throughout our lives; no matter how big or small an event or job it may have been, nothing is ever wasted, as we learn something new every day.

Chapter 31

In July 1981 when I was eight months pregnant Raymond and I received an invitation to attend the Queen's garden party at Buckingham Palace to celebrate the year of the disabled. My brother Laurie read the letter to us. We practically collapsed on the couch together in total shock and we were speechless. It was formal dress so I wore a lovely turquoise smock dress with white accessories and Raymond wore his tuxedo.

No cameras of any kind were allowed in the palace so our plan was to have a couple of photos taken at home before we left by our next door neighbour Sue, but unfortunately something went wrong with the camera and Raymond's tux had to go back the following morning so that was that: no photos to show. It was a long journey and an expensive one; just as well we had some savings put away. It was all very exciting as we had never been to London before and still couldn't believe that we were actually going to Buckingham Palace to meet the Queen.

When we arrived in London, for some unknown reason the buses that were hired to take us to the palace failed to turn up so everyone was rushing around daft trying to find a taxi; it was a total nightmare. I honestly thought we weren't going to get there when all of a sudden this guy gave a big whistle and flagged one down for us as I think he realised the position we were in. By the time we arrived at the palace there were already hundreds in the grounds waiting. The only downside for us was that we weren't allowed to take a guide with us which did make it a little difficult and also meant we missed out on a lot of things. As we entered inside the palace I got a shock when a guardsman approached me as I didn't expect it. "Would madam please take my arm," he said, "and I will escort and guide you through and into her Majesty's private garden." The same applied to Raymond and to all those who needed help and support in one way or another.

It was so lovely how it was done that I was lapping it up and enjoying every minute of it and although the sun wasn't out it was still a very hot and murky sort of day and the sweat was running off me. There were lots of tables and chairs set out in the garden and an open marquee where drinks and food were being served – that was definitely my first stop off as I was starving and dying for a drink, then a couple there came to our rescue and guided us in the right direction.

The service at the counter was marvellous considering that there were hundreds of people there. The waitresses were very well trained; everyone at all times was addressed as sir or madam which made the day extra special. She handed us both a plate with food on and a cup of tea. I was really looking forward to this. When we both sat down to eat though my jaw dropped – there was barely enough to feed a mouse; just a few tiny little fancies on the plate and I mean tiny, which only took a few seconds to eat and digest. We were still quite hungry and wanted to go back up for seconds but were worried in case the same waitress saw us and thought we were being greedy so we thought we'd better not.

Just then there was talk that the Queen and the Royal Family would be coming out very shortly to join everyone. You could feel the atmosphere changing, everyone was so excited and patiently waiting for them to appear at the top of the stairs. Many decided to move forward to the front most likely hoping to meet the Queen as she came down the stairs and into the garden. We were right down the bottom end and decided to stay put as there were people and garden furniture everywhere and we didn't want any accidents. Everyone clapped when they appeared. It was still very warm but also heavy and humid and within five to ten minutes of them being in the garden the heavens opened, and I mean opened! It wasn't just torrential, it was a monsoon. People were running all over the place for shelter but there was nowhere to go, the marquee may have been long but it wasn't very deep and it was filled in a matter of seconds.

So there we were standing getting soaking wet, not knowing where to go or what to do. I hadn't even brought a jacket with me as it was so hot and never thought for one minute to bring an umbrella and there were still another two hours to go as the party had just begun. Raymond began to panic a little as all the tables and chairs were quickly removed from the garden and because of my condition, with being huge and eight months pregnant, he was concerned with me having nowhere to sit, getting soaking wet and that it may cause some problems for both me and the baby.

He was always a born worrier where I was concerned which was lovely knowing that he cared so much about me but as usual I just laughed it off and told him not to be daft and that I was fine and then started to make a joke about it all. "Can you imagine if I went into labour here and the baby was born in Buckingham Palace?" I said. "That would certainly be a turn up for the books and would probably go down in history but Raymond didn't see it as funny like I did. We were both very grateful when two older women came to our rescue and offered their help. They took us under their wing for the rest of the afternoon and made sure we didn't miss out on anything and also gave us shelter under their brolly which was a godsend.

Later on we personally met, spoke and shook hands with the Queen, Duke of Edinburgh, Princess Margaret and the Duchess of Kent. Princess Anne passed by but still said hello to everyone. The highlight for me though was meeting Lady Diana. The Royal Family stayed out for an hour before joining some other VIPs in a large marquee. On the other hand Lady Diana decided she would stay out an extra hour because of her getting married to Charles the following week as she wanted to meet as many of the public who had come along that day and also to give a red rose to every elderly gentleman to help commemorate her wedding day. Everyone was excited and welcomed her with open arms.

Lady Diana then stopped to speak to an elderly gentleman who was standing next to me and when she gave him a red rose he was so overjoyed and couldn't stop thanking her for it. I was that engrossed in their conversation that I got such a shock when she suddenly grasped both of my hands together and held them firmly in hers while she had a chat with me. Even though it was pouring with rain she made time for everyone and captured all of our hearts. The whole day from beginning to end was the most marvellous experience ever and the opportunity of a lifetime which I will never forget as long as I live.

Chapter 32

As time drew near to having the baby I was still buzzing with energy and carried out all my daily chores as usual even with my big bump being there. Apart from us being so excited and patiently waiting for the new arrival so was everyone else including my mum, which meant a lot to the both of us.

Our big day eventually arrived on the 21st of August 1981 when I gave birth to a bouncing baby boy weighing eight pounds four ounces. He was olive skinned and had a mop of jet black hair that stood up on end and almond-shaped eyes. Raymond stayed with me right throughout the birth and we were both on cloud nine and couldn't believe that he was ours. We named him Lee Anthony Gaetano after Raymond and his Granda Deponio. I was both shocked and thrilled when Raymond's mam and sister Gloria walked in later that day and said "Hiya Kirsty." I couldn't believe that they had travelled all the way down from Edinburgh by train to see us. They brought us many gifts for Lee and a beautiful bouquet of red roses and chocolates – they were always so kind and thoughtful about everything which meant a lot to me.

My mam and dad were also very excited about seeing Lee. At first my mam was dumbstruck and was sure we had been given the wrong baby as he looked totally Chinese she said, but I reassured her that he was definitely ours as he had never left my side since he was born. The first eight hours after Lee was born he was as good as gold and slept most of the time, but after that he certainly made his mark by letting everyone know that he was there. He virtually never slept night or day and would maybe quieten down for half an hour here and there. I was put into a four-bed bay which I shared with three other mums and their babies. I don't think we proved to be very popular with them or the others elsewhere and I don't blame them as Lee's cries were so loud and would go on and on for ages. You couldn't seem to stop him once he'd started no matter how much you tried; there was just no pacifying him. He kept everyone awake and had all the babies screaming, not just in our bay but also in the others. He certainly had a good pair of lungs and made sure he used them but because of him crying so much the nurses and I were unable to get enough food down him so they had to keep me in nine days rather than seven as he had lost too much weight. The doctors then checked him over again to make sure that everything was alright, which it was.

The nurses explained that there are some babies for unknown reasons that take longer to settle down than others "and unfortunately it looks like Lee's going to be one of them" because no matter how much the nurses even tried he was exactly the same with them – which made me feel better knowing that it wasn't just me. All the nurses still loved him though and thought he was a right little character. When he was peaceful he was gorgeous, but we loved him no matter what; to us he was just perfect and we were so proud to be his mam and dad. We couldn't wait for the day to take him home so that we could be a proper little family. All I could think of was that he belonged to us and nobody could ever take him away.

He had already brought so much joy into our lives, even though he was only days old, we couldn't imagine our lives without him. We decided to put Lee's cot in our room as it was exceptionally large. Also we felt safer with him being beside us as the other room was much further away and off the sitting area.

A few weeks went by and Lee still hadn't settled down. I felt as if I was never away from the doctors as I was so worried about him and felt there was something wrong, but they reassured me that he was a very healthy baby and that everything was fine. To me it just didn't seem normal somehow for a baby so young to constantly cry as much as he did and to be so restless and awake most of the time with no reason; it just didn't add up. Just as well I had the patience of Job!

I only ever had one visit from a health visitor and that was when Lee was four weeks old and that was only because I had phoned her myself asking her to come out and see us as I felt there was a need to. After that I never saw a health visitor again. I literally walked the floors night and day and there were times I would be vomiting as I felt so ill due to the lack of sleep. Sometimes I could be on and off for over six hours just trying to get a couple of ounces of milk into him. Again it just wasn't normal – he would be screaming as if he was in terrible pain of some kind and seemed to find it difficult to suck. Whenever Lee settled down for half an hour or more so would I.

Raymond was as good as gold, always helping wherever he could. I worried about him as he was also suffering from lack of sleep and worked long hours, but he never complained. We made a great team and always worked hand in hand together in everything we did. My mam and dad were also great and absolutely adored Lee and would look after him every other weekend to help give us a break so that we could catch up with some sleep and chores.

The change in my mam's attitude and behaviour towards Raymond and me since we'd had Lee was just so good and unbelievable, she became this different person altogether and was a total joy to be with which made me feel so happy. They also had the patience of Job and walked the floors with Lee which again made me feel better knowing the problem didn't just lie with me because of him being my first-born. I was always used to children and I practically brought myself up and had always looked after my two younger brothers and sister from a very early age; even though I was still just a child myself it always seemed like second nature to me and I loved playing mother.

When Lee was about seven to eight weeks old the doctor diagnosed that he was suffering from severe colic and thrush and prescribed some medication for it as well as some vallergan which was a mild form of valium. The doctor himself was now becoming concerned about Lee's sleep pattern and felt that the vallergan would help to calm and relax him as he didn't want Lee to exhaust himself which could have led to many other problems. We were both so relieved that something was going to be done to help him as we knew there was a problem as it was no ordinary cry – and as mothers we know the difference.

It took a good month or two before the medication for the colic and thrush really kicked in, after that the change in Lee was amazing. He was now becoming a very happy little boy and was enjoying his food immensely. He now started to sleep for longer periods through the day, but come early evening and through the night it was a different kettle of fish altogether.

Chapter 33

A club for the blind was set up in Gateshead in 1978 of which we were members of. Most of the members were years older than us but we still enjoyed it anyway as it was a night out. We mainly played cards and dominoes and would also have a chat with others and exchange jokes. On an odd occasion I would take my guitar in and we would have a good old sing along.

It would be around November 1981 when I received a telephone call from our social worker Ralph Harrison asking if Raymond and I would be interested in becoming part of an athletics team for the blind in Gateshead if such a team was set up. *Wow,* I thought, as sport was right up my street. I was all for it, raring to go and couldn't wait for the first meeting. Apparently Ralph had received a visit from a young cockney girl called Doreen who was a couple of years younger than me and was also blind. She had recently moved up from London to start her new life living here in Gateshead with her seven year old son. She was a sportswoman herself and had been a member of the blind athletics team in London and had called in to our local social services to find out where and when our athletics team met in Gateshead as she felt it was important for her to carry on with her sporting career. Doreen said she was totally horrified and dumbfounded when she found out that we didn't have a team here in the North East but also that social services hadn't even heard of such games before and thought that they were all living in the dark ages up here. So without further ado Ralph Harrison our social worker arranged our first meeting that same November in 1981.

Raymond and I, along with Ralph Sample who was also one of the younger blind members from our Gateshead club, went along to hear Doreen give us a talk about how the blind athletics worked. She had a great sense of humour and won us over, so within no time the Gateshead visually handicapped sports and recreational club was founded. The four of us began our training that coming January 1982 at the Gateshead Stadium in Felling. Ralph Sample was already a member there and had been for quite some time. He was a bit of a sportsman himself and mainly trained in powerlifting but also knew a lot about the field events and offered to coach us. Also, with Ralph being in the know, he approached some of the professional coaches he knew there asking if they would be willing and kind enough to offer some of their time coaching us in running and providing some back-up in the field events. Ralph felt it was going to be too much for him to do on his own as he said you do need a pair of eyes around as well. Apparently Stan Long was the only coach who came forward out of all those Ralph had asked; he was one of the top running coaches in the North East and had trained many big sporting stars such as Brendan Foster and Steve Cram.

Stan was a right character, an absolute great guy and one in a million. Nothing was ever a problem to him; he even went out of his way to help us with the field events as best as he possibly could as well as coaching us in running. At first we started out with only four in our team, so Ralph Harrison, the secretary of our club, kindly offered his free time and took us in his own personal car so that we could compete in the blind athletic games. He was also a very genuine and lovely man who encouraged and believed in us; nothing was ever a problem as he was always there, willing and eager by offering a helping hand wherever he could and he became a great friend to all of us.

That same year we were very fortunate enough to have had donated a minibus for our athletics club which was a total godsend and a marvellous asset. This now meant that our team could grow by inviting other blind and partially sighted people along to come and join us, so by the end of the season that year we had built up to seven. We travelled to different parts of the country and had competed in the UK championships at Glasgow, the national games at Manchester and the rotary international games at Stoke Mandeville.

It had been the most marvellous experience and fantastic first year for all of us as well as for Gateshead as we brought back home many trophies and medals with us for the Borough. Altogether that year I had won five medals – one gold, three silver and a bronze – along with six other trophies. This was for the shot-put, discus, javelin and both high and long jump. Before the season finished in September I was approached by a couple of the top organizers of the games. They expressed how thrilled they had been with my performances and achievements considering that it was only my first year at the games. They then said if I trained hard enough over the next six months in time for the national games the following year, in 1983, they believed I could vastly improve my performances and if I did there was every possibility that I could achieve the standards to be accepted on to the British squad team to represent Great Britain in the 1984 Paralympics in Los Angeles.

With me being new to the games I was really taken aback by what they had said as I had never heard of the Paralympics before and never thought for one minute that the disabled held their own – and especially in the same year and country as the ordinary Olympics. *Wow, what an achievement and honour that would be if I were ever fortunate enough to qualify and get through,* I thought. I had always been a keen sportsperson from being young at school and loved a challenge, but mainly looked forward to taking part every year and was always eager to give everything a try. So, once again it was back to the grindstone!

I found it encouraging when I had something to focus on as it made me set more goals. Somehow I felt as if I always needed something to keep me motivated and to keep a spring in my step in order for me to cope and get on with life, but more so to give hope and encouragement to others that life is about living, enjoying and moving forward without allowing ourselves to keep falling back to where we once were. So all I kept telling myself now was, *watch out Los Angeles because here I come.* You have to believe that everything is possible and if I didn't make it, it wouldn't be the end of the world; it's not always about winning, it's about taking part and knowing that you've given it your all and best shot ever. That's what it's all about!

Chapter 34

Lee was growing up so fast. He was just over a year old when the first year of the games had finished and we didn't know where the time had gone. He was a right little character and a proper boy, always full of the joys of spring and had bags of energy. We just adored and loved him to bits and felt so proud to be his parents and I still couldn't believe that he was our son and a part of both of us.

Although the doctors managed to get on top of Lee's problems and pain by the time he was almost four months old, they had still never managed to help with his sleep pattern. I remember one day someone mentioning the word hyperactivity to me and thought maybe that's what Lee had. I had never heard of the word before and knew nothing about it so I thought I would mention it to my doctor, but he just laughed and said there was no such thing and it was a load of nonsense. Of course with me being so young and naive I thought if anyone would know it would be the doctor and just accepted what he said.

Our first Christmas together with Lee was just wonderful and the most perfect and best day ever. We spent it with my mam and dad and the rest of the family as she had asked us to stay over – they were just as excited as we were in having a new baby in the house especially with it being Christmas Day. It was hard to tell who the biggest child was that day as we were all like big kids when it came to opening Lee's presents and playing with them, especially the Fisher-Price xylophone. That was the best. He was only four and a half months old and hadn't a clue what was going on, but at the end of the day we are all still children at heart, no matter how old we may be.

At the age of six months Lee began to crawl, but not the

ordinary way, on his hands and knees, like I expected him to, which I suppose shouldn't have surprised me. Instead he was like a gorilla on four paws with both his arms and legs straight and his bottom in the air. He was solid, strong as an ox and moved like lightning; there was no stopping him now and our work was certainly cut out for us. I decided to go and buy a little bell from the pet shop – the kind that you would hang in a bird cage. This was another one of Sheila Tyrell's great tips (the woman I had met at the guide dog centre). I slotted some ribbon through and would tie it on the straps of his dungarees and little suits as best as I could so when he moved around I would know where he was.

We both thought now that he was crawling it would help him to sleep at night as it would tire him out. What a joke that was. I think we were being too optimistic or maybe living in hope. I had never come across anyone that had as much energy as Lee did; he was happier than ever now that he was on the move, you just couldn't keep him still.

I'll never forget the night the cot collapsed with Lee in it. He would have been about eight to ten months old and I have to say I wasn't surprised one little bit when it happened. As usual he was jumping up and down, rocking and shaking the cot trying to find a way out. We were trying so hard to get to sleep when all of a sudden we heard in the distance...ping, what on Earth was that. Immediately we jumped out of bed to see to him.

I nearly died when I bent over the cot and couldn't find him, I tried to undo the safety locks so I could pull the cot side down but it was jammed and wouldn't move as both ends of the cot had loosened and were tilting inwards. The mattress had burst through the mesh base at the bottom, tilting it, making it almost like a slide and had taken Lee down with it.

Well, you can imagine the commotion and carry on we had that night trying to get him out. We kept talking to him and made fun of it all so that he wouldn't get upset, move or make matters worse. Instead he just sat there as good as gold waiting patiently for us to get him out. I know it may be difficult to believe but it's true: as young as he was, somehow he always seemed to understand whenever there was a problem he had to be good, as he was well tuned in and knew that we couldn't see. Even when I spoon-fed him in his high chair he would automatically hold my hand and guide it to his mouth and even when Raymond and I were looking for things by feeling and fumbling about, again Lee would automatically bring items to us even if they weren't the right ones. It was just amazing how he did it and he would be overjoyed when we praised him.

We eventually managed to get Lee out safe and sound but what a struggle it was. So here we all were, 4:30 in the morning, wide awake, Lee in his play pen playing with his toys while Raymond and I were scouting around on our hands and knees searching for the missing nuts, bolts and screws. We purposely took Lee out of the way as we didn't want any more problems that night as he was terrible for putting small things into his mouth no matter how many times you told him not to. My divan skills certainly came in handy that night in putting the cot back together and also repairing the spring base. When we finished we both sat down and laughed over a cup of tea, seeing the funny side of what had just happened and thought it was another little story to add to the list to tell Lee about when he was older.

Chapter 35

In 1981 in Norway a small group of blind Scandinavians were about to reveal a sport with a difference to the whole world. The team came up with a simple idea of putting a small bleeping device into a rugby ball and to form a smaller pitch as well as playing different pieces of music from the goalpost areas that they felt would enable the blind to play a remarkable and great game of rugby. The result of the game had been such a great success in Norway that 59 year old Emlyn Stordahl, who was blind and was the brains behind it all, decided he wanted to come to Britain to find and recruit another blind team to play international games against his own country.

So in June 1982 Emlyn and his team of coaches who were all blind arrived in Britain for the first time and they were also about to take their first steps towards launching rugby here in our little town of Gateshead; how awesome is that? They were looking for volunteers, so a few of us blind local athletes went along to try it out, along with Stewart a blind athlete from York who also came up to join us. They took us through all the basics and wanted to see how well we handled the bleeping ball as their plans were to return that September to stage and hold the first official blind rugby match here in good old Gateshead.

The match took place locally at the Low Fell rugby ground and we were to play the game exactly the same way as they did back in Norway. The weather wasn't too bad; it was dry but I still found it quite chilly. I suppose the big professionals would have said it was the most perfect day for a match but no doubt I would soon warm up once I started running about. I had never played a game of rugby before except for the small taster session we had had in June which was mainly learning the skills of the game and about handling and passing the ball. So, once again this was going to be another great experience and challenge, not only for me, but for all of us really.

There were five to a team and each side wore different textured strips so that by touch we'd be able to tell who the opposition was. What made this game so exceptional and special was that it was thought to have been the first blind rugby match ever to have been played in Britain and not only was I the first blind female to have played rugby but I was also the first female to have ever played with an all-male team. Five of us players were from Gateshead, four from York, along with Emlyn from Norway.

Pop music was blasted out from one end of the pitch and Dr Who from the other which was obviously done that way to guide each team in the right direction of play. I thought it was tough when I had done karate and free fighting but this game of rugby we played was way beyond everything I had ever done and experienced. It was actually the toughest and most terrifying sport I had ever undertaken, and believe you me there was no exception whatsoever made from any of the guys including Raymond for having a girl on board. I was charged into at full speed and thought I had been hit by a bulldozer, then I was thrown around like a rag doll, tackled to the ground and to top it all off I felt as if I had been jumped and trampled on by a herd of elephants because that's exactly what it felt like when they were all lying on top of me. I honestly don't know how I walked away without any injuries as there was one particular time I thought I had broken every bone in my body as I couldn't move an inch. I didn't feel I was going to be able to stand up let alone walk again and carry on, but after a few minutes or more, I managed to pick myself up and finish the match.

The Norwegians were thrilled with our performance and I have to say so was I with mine. I might have been a pushover at the beginning and held back a little but once I found my feet after being battered and thrown about it was time to show the guys just what us girls were made of. So I began to put an extra bit of girl power into the game, letting them know I meant business and gave out as good as I got.

I think most of the guys had scored tries but by gum so had I – three to be precise. No matter how hard they tried to catch or take me down they failed miserably. I've often wondered what their thoughts were after being outrun and fought back against by a girl especially when it's classed as the macho man's game. I felt wonderful and on top of the world to be exact, as I showed them just what girl power was that day. On the day of the match we all pulled together and gave it our best shot by using all of our skills to the best of our ability. Not only had we proved to ourselves that such a game like this could be done but also to everyone else out there.

So please, again, remember no matter what disability you may have, how big or small, always believe that everything is possible. So get up and go!

Chapter 36

Raymond and I were very much outdoor people and Lee was becoming the same. Although he enjoyed playing with his toys he could only concentrate on them for a short period of time before he wanted to be on the move again. Most days he would crawl to the sitting room door, pull himself up and start making noises and begin to bang on it with his hands. He may have still been young and unable to speak but he always made himself understood to us – this one meaning that he wanted to be outside. Even though he loved the freedom of being able to get about, he was also very happy and content to sit outside in his pram at the front door which was great as it enabled me to catch up with some chores. He really enjoyed just sitting there watching everyone go by and loved it when they stopped to talk to him.

Raymond used to tell me stories about when he was young and how his parents used to take them all away when they were children on day trips to different places despite them not having a lot of money and about how much fun they all had together. Hearing that used to really bring it home to me and would sometimes leave me with a tear in my eye and a lump in my throat wishing that I had some lovely memories like that to remember. So now that we had Lee we both felt it was very important for us to spend as much time together as a family as we possibly could.

Quite often at night when Raymond came home from work he would down his tea, have a quick shower and as long as it wasn't pouring down with rain we'd wrap Lee up according to the weather, put him in his pram and off we'd go to Saltwell Park. It was about a twenty minute walk from where we lived and what a beautiful place it was; I believe it was classed as one of the best in the country. There was lots to see and do as it had a large boating lake with plenty of swans in it and there was a small pets corner. In the autumn and spring the park gates closed earlier so it meant we could only spend an hour there because of us arriving so late.

I was always well prepared and would have everything that I needed for Lee with me. So after leaving the park we didn't see the point in rushing back home as it didn't matter what time we tried to put Lee down he would still be wide awake till yon time in the morning so we always made a night of it and went for a good old walk about. We'd first go up to Low Fell then make our way to Sheriff Hill where we'd stop and get some fish and chips and then eat them on the way back down to Deckham and then to Cemetery Road, which was quite an all-round journey. Sometimes we didn't get back till ten or maybe eleven at night, but what the heck, we thoroughly enjoyed ourselves and got some exercise and fresh air at the same time.

Lee was as happy as Larry sitting up and watching all the traffic go by; to us that's all that mattered – as long as he was happy then so were we. Sometimes it would be a quick bath for him when we got in or maybe a top and tail and I would give him a bath in the morning. Raymond used to work alternate weekends and what we loved more than anything else was spending all day in Saltwell Park, especially in the summer, as we didn't need to go anywhere else as there was something for everyone from tennis courts, bowling greens, crazy golf, play areas and much more, even a small shop which sold hot and cold food. There were also plenty of picnic tables to sit at which were placed around in different areas on the most beautiful lawns with plenty of room for families to lie about and play games. We took toys, our own picnic and a large blanket to sit on and would have the time of our life with Lee; he enjoyed the freedom, fresh air and so did we.

It was very important to us that Lee missed out on nothing, especially because of our loss of sight, and so we tried to bring him

CHAPTER 36

up in a normal environment as best as we could. After all it was a sighted world he lived in and belonged to. Both Raymond and I were very independent, versatile and mobile people and we were determined to keep it that way. It was also very important to us that we made sure we always fitted in with society and still remained part of our sighted world as well.

You might find it strange that I have made such a statement like that but it's true. I had mixed with lots of people from different backgrounds of disabilities including my own who had been quite happy to cut themselves off from society and would prefer themselves and their children to live in their own little world of their own kind. I'm certainly not condemning them because it's each to their own, but it wasn't for us and most certainly not what we wanted for our children. We just enjoyed the simple things in life which didn't cost the earth to do and as long as we had each other, our little bundle of joy and enough to get us by, that's all that mattered and nothing else.

Chapter 37

When Raymond came down here to live we often went into Gateshead and we always made a point of going to Boots the Chemist where I first worked when I was able to see. It always brought back many happy memories and some funny ones. The shop was exactly the same then but over the years it has changed dramatically– and I can't say it was for the best as I loved it the old way. There were a lot of the same staff still there and I used to enjoy having a natter with them.

It was a very busy shop when I worked there and on a Saturday it would be mayhem, especially on the record department and on fancy goods which was where I used to work. At the time each department had their own appointed head and Mrs Peed was ours. She was about five foot six, slim build with short dark hair and glasses. She was lovely and everyone got on well with her. It was the days of flower power, mini skirts, stockings and suspender belts as well as great music like the Beatles, Rolling Stones, The Kinks, Amen Corner, Love Affair and many more. 'Je t'aime' was one of the most sexiest records to have ever been released then and it was the talk of the nation but also great to listen to.

We had a small toy section and the biggest attraction for the children were the small matchbox and corgi cars; there were about 76 to collect and they came in a small presentation box priced at two and six. Brass, copper and sixties glassware were very popular and wearing rings was all the range. We had counters with dozens and dozens of trays filled with them; it was mainly just cheap costume jewellery but still very good quality. They came in all shapes and sizes and with the most beautiful coloured glass and stones in them. Some started from as little as one and six and could go up to as much as five shillings which is equal to 25 pence today and was worth quite a bit then taking into consideration your weekly pay. I earned four pounds and four shillings a week and in 1969 that was a good wage and a considerable amount of money. It certainly went further then and you could do and buy more with it. My mam would give me a pound back out of my wages and that would be my pocket money for the week and I can't begin to tell you how rich I felt on that day.

If you are young and reading this book you may be laughing and I don't blame you, but it's true and it's not as if the sixties and seventies were classed as the olden days, it was far from it. So let me tell you exactly what I spent my pound pocket money on in a week and just how far it stretched compared to today.

It paid for my weekly bus fares travelling to and from work as well as all my meals, teas and snacks each day from the Boots canteen which altogether came to twelve shillings, leaving me eight. This was enough to pay for my karate lesson, go to the pictures, buy my sweets, a packet of cigarettes and also a little something left to put in my bottles for savings.

Now how about that? Not bad, eh!

I must tell you about the most embarrassing experience I had whilst working there. It was my third day and I had started on the pharmacy department. Louie the head of department was off, leaving Linda in charge. She was a few years older than me and we got on like a house on fire.

She reminded me very much of Dusty Springfield, she Looked the double of her, was the same height, build, hairstyle, colouring and even down to the thick black eye-shadow and pan-stick on her face. Linda thought because it was reasonably quiet in the shop that it would be a good time for her to go upstairs and bring some new stock down and that it would also be a good opportunity to see how I managed the counter on my own. I was really chuffed with myself and was managing everything without a pick of bother until this young man walked in. He'd be roughly about 26 or 27; he walked suavely over to the counter as cool as a cucumber and just stood there.

"Can I help you, sir?" I said. Mr Crowder our manager was very strict about how we approached our customers, and quite right too. It always had to be sir or madam and nothing else. "Could I have a packet of Fetherlites, love?" he replied.

Oh, I thought to myself as I hadn't heard of them before, so I immediately turned around to face the back shelves on the wall to have a look. There was a huge area to cover and literally dozens and dozens of bottles and boxes of medication to go through. I hadn't a clue where to start so I began to look through the meds for headaches, sore throats, colds and so on. I was trying to look so confident and professional as if I knew what I was doing and had worked there for ages. Linda always told me if I was stuck about anything just go and see the pharmacist or simply ask the customer again the name of the product and what they were taking or using it for as it would give me a better idea where to look for it. So that's exactly what I did.

I couldn't believe the change in the man's face; he was speechless and just stood there saying nothing. I didn't see the problem; it was no big deal – all I wanted to know was what he used them for. There were about thirty drawers or more behind me underneath the shelves, stretching from one end of the counter to the other. They were all in alphabetical order and all held the smaller items such as aspirin, Codis, Fiery Jack, Vaseline and so on. There was a card in each one explaining what was inside. I immediately thought that's where they must be as I couldn't find them anywhere on the back shelves. I then looked down the card and found everything bar this damn pack of Fetherlites.

I turned round to apologise to the man and explained that I was having difficulty in finding them, but by this time he looked in a right flap and was tapping his hands on the counter. I was just about to go and seek some help from the pharmacist when all of a sudden I caught a glimpse of Mr Crowder the manager over on the beauty counter. He was a lovely man who treated everyone with great respect, no matter what age they were. He was average height and build and always well presented; he had a mop of jet black, wavy hair brushed back, a moustache and a huge smile which nobody could miss. I'm not too sure how old he was – he may have been in his mid-thirties – but I have to say that he was a very handsome man. I put my hand in the air and shouted over to grab his attention. He was only about twenty feet away and as he slowly walked over I started to explain the difficulty I was having in finding this so called medication and how I wasn't too sure what it was for. All of a sudden there was this panicked look on his face then luckily Linda appeared on the shop floor with the stock. *Thank goodness*, I thought, as I was so relieved. Then Mr Crowder dashed over to her, whispered something, looked round and pointed my way.

You should have seen the look on her face. *What on earth's wrong with everybody*, I thought. I was beginning to feel very embarrassed and uncomfortable, not just for me but also for the poor man. He was just standing there totally dumbfounded by it all; no wonder, he probably thought we were all nuts. I certainly did because of everyone's behaviour. If that had been me I think I would have walked out of the shop long before now. Then Linda dashed over, dragged me down on the floor behind the counter and said, "Do you not know what they are? They're Durex!"

"What!" I shouted. I was totally gobsmacked and my eyes nearly popped out of my head. I was horrified! I explained that I had already asked what he used them for. I didn't even have the courage to stand up and face him again, so Linda did while I still sat on the floor. We never saw hide nor hair of him again and I'm not surprised. I laugh about it now and so do many others when I tell the tale.

Chapter 38

When Lee was about six months old, Susan and David, our
downstairs neighbours, were talking about moving and had already
started looking for a property to buy. We had all moved in roughly
about the same time and they now had a little girl called Kay who
was just gorgeous. She had a lovely personality and was very quiet
and gentle like her dad. Susan was just the opposite and whenever
she was around there was never a dull moment. We all got on well
together and she always made us laugh. We had also dreamt over
the years about owning our own little house one day and having a
garden to sit out in. At the time we had never given much thought
about leaving Cemetery Road as we were still very happy and
content living there. It wasn't until Susan and Dave started viewing
some properties that it brought it home and I began to realise just
what a miss they would all be and also that Lee wouldn't have a
friend to play with and grow up with, which really bothered me and
made me feel quite unsettled.

Looking back, if Susan, or anyone else for that matter, had
told me that in a matter of weeks I would also have been making
a decision to move, I would never have believed them, yet that's
exactly what happened. Raymond was dead easy going and when I
discussed it with him, he said as long as I was happy then so was he.

It's so strange how things happen and to think that's all it took,
just something as small as that, to trigger me off and make me want
to get up and go after our little dream house too. We were very
good savers and already had quite a bit put away and my maternity
grant and superannuation rebate had upped things very nicely, but
it still meant we had to put every penny away possible if we were to
succeed. We hadn't a clue where we wanted to move to and because

Raymond wasn't familiar with the areas down here he left the decision with me. My mam suggested that we move back to Lobley Hill as she thought if we ever needed her to babysit then we'd be right on the doorstep and no travelling would be involved which would make life easier for Raymond and I and less time-consuming. She certainly had a valid point and it made a lot of sense but even the smallest of houses in Lobley Hill were just a little more than we could afford as the mortgage rates were quite high at the time, making the monthly repayments out of our reach.

Apart from that we would still have to put down quite a hefty deposit as most people had to in those days, as mortgages were given based on the husband's income only and nothing else. We were both very cautious people and I had never taken on any debt before; what we didn't have we did without until we had saved up enough money and paid cash for it. So this was a huge step forward for us and if we had any doubts about anything and thought we couldn't afford it we wouldn't even contemplate on going there. We did view some older properties elsewhere that were in our price range but weren't very nice at all. After much thought we decided that Lobley Hill ticked all the boxes and was where we wanted to be, but we would have to wait patiently and hope that the mortgage rates would come down enough for us to just afford one of the small basic Leech semis.

Lobley Hill was a very friendly community and a nice place to live and of course I still knew a lot of people and was very familiar with the area as well as being near my family so it would be kind of like going back home. Just after Lee's first birthday in August the mortgage rates came crashing down which meant we were now in a position to buy and began house hunting straight away. We were so excited and couldn't believe our luck. The first two we viewed in Lobley Hill were pretty disappointing, more so one of them – you would have thought it had been ransacked. It was that bad we even phoned the agents up to let them know the situation in case they thought we had done it. There was that much rubble and paper on the sitting room floor that you couldn't even walk through it. It was disgusting!

A few days later my dad had gone up to the top shops and on his way back down saw a small sign in a window saying 'house for sale' and the number to ring. We got on the phone to the owner immediately and made arrangements to meet her the following day. She hadn't lived in the property for about two years but as soon as we walked in we knew that this was the one as we had the same feeling as when we walked in to Cemetery Road and we fell in love with it straight away. It was a small two bed semi-detached, no passageway and had a small sitting room and a small diner with a little kitchen. It had a separate toilet and bathroom with a large bedroom at the front and a smaller one at the back. It was a pre-war house with a small garden at the front and a side alleyway led to a larger garden at the back.

There was quite a bit of work to be done but it had great potential. Although the front door and downstairs window had been replaced the rest of them needed to be done as soon as possible as they were all old wrought iron ones. There was no central heating, the fire was a death trap which needed gutting, and the house needed decorating and rewiring throughout as there was still quite a few of the two pin point sockets there.

The asking price was thirteen and a half thousand. We were first time buyers but the building society would only allow us eleven thousand and seven hundred pounds for our mortgage which was fine as we had the extra deposit to put down. So we stood in real good stead and offered her the full amount as we didn't want to lose it because it was just everything we had dreamt of and wanted it so badly. We were so thrilled that she accepted our offer as there was another couple coming to view it after us.

Within no time our mortgage came through, but while we were still waiting for everything to be finalised the owner left the keys with our adjoining neighbours so that we had access to the property so we could take the necessary workers in to make plans for the jobs we wanted them to undertake. It was so exciting, the thought of starting all over again; I think it was because it was our first house that we were buying together and knowing that it was going to be ours. We felt so lucky, a dream come true and we were on cloud nine about it all.

Ann and Eddie, our next door neighbours to be, were just great. They had three children, Gillian, David, and then Natalie who was just six weeks older than Lee which we were so pleased about, knowing that he would have someone to play with. They were all lovely children and we couldn't wait to move in and hopefully get to know them better. Our plans were to take the wall down between the kitchen and dining area so we could make it into a much larger one, renewing all the doors, decorate throughout and to carry out all the major jobs that desperately needed doing. Obviously this was going to take the best part of our money up, but because I was a very cautious person I made sure that a tidy little sum was put away to one side for an emergency in case anything happened – as you never know what lies around the corner.

Everything was finalised by November the 5th and we were now the proud owners of 44 Rothbury Gardens. We lived on a main street and bus route and had sunshine from morning till night. The shops were just yards away, the school right opposite and we had the most spectacular view looking over to Gateshead, Low Fell and Newcastle – and at night it looked like fairy land when all the lights were on. What more could anyone ask for? I remembered the view very well from when I could see as I passed there twice a day on my way to school, never thinking for one minute that one day I would be living there with the man of my dreams and our precious baby boy.

We were so lucky that the rent was very low at Cemetery Road as it meant we could still afford to live there until all the work was carried out at our new house. This gave us plenty of time to pack and clean up at our own leisure. We set the date for moving in on February the 8th 1983 as all the work was finished and we were ready to go. Susan and Dave were thrilled for us both but we felt quite sad that they still hadn't managed to find a place yet considering that they had been looking for much longer than we had and we hoped they would find something soon.

When it came to the crunch in leaving I was so surprised at just how excited I was about moving into our new home and back to Lobley Hill as we had lived at Cemetery Road for over six and a half years. We had loved every minute of being there and had nothing but wonderful memories but life changes and I knew it was time for us to move on and we would take all of those wonderful and happy cherished memories with us.

Chapter 39

It was a blizzard of snow when we moved in and I couldn't believe the amount of boxes we had. It's amazing how much you collect over the years and I was a right hoarder.

Lee was almost eighteen months old at the time and he made himself at home immediately. We had already brought him up with us on a number of occasions so that he would be familiar with the surroundings and would help to settle him in, which he did with no bother. In many ways we were both just glad to be there as we had also never stopped working on the house over the last three months with doing one thing or another.

As well as all the travelling up and down on the buses we sometimes didn't get back till yon time at night, thick with muck and freezing cold as it was winter. Raymond and I were never shy of hard work or afraid of getting our hands dirty; we would get stuck in and give anything a try as we always loved a challenge. We stripped all the walls ourselves by hand from top to bottom, which believe you me took some doing as it was wood chip paper throughout and I don't know how many coats of paint they had on them.

So, you can imagine the fun we had in getting it off. I believe that there were special steamers out to help with stripping walls but unfortunately at the time we hadn't heard of them. So for us it was just a bucket of water, a pasting brush and your good old metal scrapers. We also prepared all the walls as there was a lot of polyfillering and sanding down to be done as they were old and crumbling in places. There was also plenty of muck to clean up and washing down to do especially after the workers finished their jobs as thick dust seemed to travel everywhere, so it was always important for us to keep on top of it all.

Although we were now in we still had another long day ahead of us unpacking, sorting boxes out as well as putting furniture together. We didn't feel under any pressure and felt we could relax a little now as we had all the time in the world to sort everything out. I'm not going to pretend that the work we did was a doddle and easy because it wasn't as we had many mishaps along the way. It probably took us three times as long as anybody else because of our circumstances as we had to keep checking the walls by feeling them over and over again to make sure that nothing and nowhere had been missed which can be very tedious, frustrating and exhausting at times.

But again the satisfaction of knowing that we had managed and succeeded in doing it was quite something else. We were always the type to never give up or let anything stand in our way and would push ourselves to the limit, no matter what.

We both feel we were very lucky to have lost our sight at such a young age, because we still had youth on our side which does seem to be a help in terms of confidence and adapting to life than for those who have lost their sight later in life, and eventually over the years everything just became second nature to us.

I'm sure the same applies to many others out there who also have a disability and even though Raymond has just the slightest vision at the corner of his eyes he is still registered and classed as blind as there is not enough sight there to be classed as partial.

I am so pleased that the Paralympic Games were held here in Britain in 2012 and received the same coverage as the ordinary Olympics had done for many years and it wasn't before time. It was the most wonderful way to portray right across the world just what everyone is capable of doing despite their disability and I just hope that the small minority of the public who have been unable to accept just what we can do without passing judgement will hopefully now be able to accept us for who we are and see us all in a different light altogether.

It had been a long day and we were ready to hit the sack. The place was looking more like home as we had most of the furniture in place. Lee's cot and our bed were put together and made up and we had managed to unpack some of the main boxes but there was still plenty more to do. The only thing that bothered me and made me feel a little strange was going upstairs to sleep as I had been so used to living downstairs, but it didn't bother Raymond one iota. We were so pleased that my mam had Lee for the night as we were shattered and were looking forward to a good night's sleep. The following morning when we came downstairs for breakfast, Raymond and I stood in the middle of the sitting room floor and hugged each other tight, as the house had the most wonderful feeling to it, just like Cemetery Road did. In many ways we felt as if we had never left there and had picked our little flat up and brought it with us; we were just so happy about everything and life itself.

We felt so rich, like millionaires to be exact, and were so grateful for everything we had. Life just seemed to be getting better and better as we had the house of our dreams, a little boy, each other and the warmth of my mam towards us now. We still felt like a couple of kids and were madly in love and felt we had the whole world at our fingertips which no amount of money could ever buy.

Raymond was still working on the Team Valley Trading Estate which was just down the road from where we lived though he had changed his job two years earlier and was now working for UBU bedding company. He loved it there and was making quite good wages with working overtime. They were really impressed with his enthusiasm at the interview and put him on a few weeks' trial and gladly offered him the job working as a labourer having to keep twenty-three divan makers supplied with all their materials. Apparently, before Raymond came along, the company had already tried six different sighted men to do the same job but unfortunately

every one of them had been unsuccessful as they couldn't manage
to keep up the pace with all the supplies, leaving many of the
tradesmen waiting for their materials – which was no good as they
all had targets to reach before going on to piece work, which meant
they would be losing out on money – this was no good to them
or the management. So, Raymond was told that because of his
determination and efficiency in proving the job could be done, this
would put things in good stead for them wanting to employ other
disabled people in the future.

Raymond worked late most nights until about six o'clock, which
meant he would arrive home at about twenty past six. He would
always phone and tell me if he was working later than that so I
wouldn't worry and knew where he was. Every night I would say to
Lee, "Where's daddy? He'll be coming home shortly from work."
I had no sooner got the words out of my mouth than he would
quickly run across the floor, jump on to Raymond's chair and look
out of the window. Nothing got past him; he understood every
word you said. We'd both be huddled on the chair together waiting
patiently for Raymond to arrive.

It was now the 8th of March and I couldn't believe that we'd been
in four weeks already. Although it was a pleasant night it was still
too cold to stand at the front door so as usual we'd both be on the
chair waiting for Raymond. Lee would be standing on the arm and
leaning forward so he could see further down the road whilst I
knelt on the seat keeping a tight hold of him.

He was always so excited and would be shouting, "Daddy come,
daddy come," but as soon as he caught a glimpse of Raymond's
red and beige checked lumber-jacket he would be down off that
chair like a shot and would run as quickly as he could across the
sitting room floor and into the kitchen where the back door was,
chuckling away to himself. It was a twelve panelled frosted glass
door but apparently you could still see people's images through
it. Lee would be literally hugging the door with his face pressed

against the pane of glass and as soon as he heard the clumping of Raymond's footsteps down the alleyway he would be jumping up and down and clapping his hands with excitement shouting, "Daddy, daddy!" He was waiting for him to tap on the glass as he always teased him and would say loudly, "Is there anybody there?" Lee would be giggling away and as soon as I opened the door he would be standing there with open arms waiting for Raymond to whisk him off his feet and put him up into the air. It was lovely to see them so happy together and it didn't matter how tired Raymond was, he always made the time to play with Lee and tell him stories.

He was an absolutely great dad and loved Lee to bits.

That night we were still waiting and it was unusual for Raymond to be late as you could literally set your watch by him as he was always spot on time. My immediate reaction was he had either been held back a few minutes or he's stopped to talk to someone on the way home. It was now twenty to seven and there was still no sign of Raymond. I was now beginning to feel a little uncomfortable and anxious as he always phoned me if he was working later than usual so that I wouldn't worry unnecessarily as he knew what I was like.

It's now ten to seven and I'm beginning to feel sick with worry and thinking all sorts as you do, you know what it's like, your mind runs away with you and somehow you just can't seem to stop it. Lee was also becoming restless and no wonder after waiting for so long, so I took him down from the chair so he could play with his toys. I was trying very hard to keep myself calm as I didn't want Lee to see me upset because as young as they are, believe you me, they also know when something's wrong. By the time it reached seven o'clock my mind was all over the place and I was feeling ill.

My gut feeling was somehow telling me that Raymond wasn't coming home that night as all I could think was that something dreadful had happened to him like being knocked over by a car.

I was becoming paranoid just thinking about it and kept telling myself not to be stupid and thinking such bad thoughts like that, but I just couldn't help it. A couple of minutes later there was a knock at the back door. I can't begin to tell you the relief I felt inside when I heard it. I jumped to my feet and was so happy and said to Lee, "Daddy's home, thank goodness he's here. Come on, let's let him in."

I would normally have let Lee go first but I was so anxious and just wanted to hear his voice knowing that he was alright. Lee followed me quickly shouting as usual "daddy daddy". He was so excited about seeing him! As I got nearer to the door I knew something wasn't quite right as I couldn't hear Raymond tapping on the glass and teasing Lee as he normally would have. So I was very reluctant to open it and asked who was there.

"It's me, Christine, your mam. Open the door, love," she said.

Straight away I knew there was something seriously wrong and began to shake and thought I was going to throw up all over the place as I didn't know what I was going to hear. I was all fingers and thumbs trying to open the lock and when I did my brother Laurie who was almost nineteen was there along with two police officers who introduced themselves to me. I was in total shock and numb from head to foot and found it difficult to speak. The police officers told me that Raymond had been knocked down on the Team Valley Trading Estate on his way home from work. They explained that they didn't know how serious his injuries were, so not "to worry too much as things mightn't be as bad as you think".

I didn't know whether to believe them or not and thought they might just be saying anything to help make me feel better. All that mattered to me was knowing that he was still alive! They dropped Lee off at my dad's and took us straight over in the police car to the Newcastle General Hospital where Raymond was. No one really spoke on the way except when one of the officers informed me how far we had travelled and that it wouldn't be long before we arrived.

My mind was whizzing round and round as so many thoughts were flashing through it. I couldn't stop thinking about how things must really be as Newcastle General was always noted for taking the worst cases in and if things weren't as bad he would've been taken up to the Queen Elizabeth Hospital which wasn't far from where the accident had happened. I found it more frightening and upsetting not knowing all the ins and outs at the time and couldn't wait to be beside him.

The hospital was only seven miles away, yet by the time we arrived I felt as if I'd been in the car for hours. We were immediately taken into a side room where we were told that a doctor would be coming to speak to us very shortly. The three of us just sat there waiting anxiously, saying very little to each other, as I think my mam and Laurie were also in shock. Deep down I had this feeling that it wasn't going to be good news but I was still trying very hard to keep calm and focussed.

The doctor eventually arrived and as he walked in I stood up and waited for him to speak. It's amazing the strength you seem to get from somewhere when you need it most of all. I thought I would have been no good, crumbled away and sobbing my heart out before now. I hadn't even cried yet; yes I'd had a few tears but that was all. Although I knew it was real and happening I also felt as if I was inside a large bubble as something like this always happens to others but not to you.

The doctor then told me that Raymond was still alive but only just and didn't know if he would last much longer as he was very critically ill and had received the most horrific multiple injuries and I was told to prepare myself for the worst. I broke out in a cold sweat, my whole body felt weird and I thought I was going to collapse. I could hear everything he was saying but it sounded as if he was talking in slow motion.

Don't go down now, Christine I kept telling myself, *don't you dare, you have to be strong for Raymond and Lee as they need you.* I honestly don't know how I managed to speak but I did and said, "But what happens if he does live? What will the outcome be?"

He replied that they hadn't looked that far ahead yet and explained that if he did – which they strongly didn't expect him to – that there was every possibility he would be brain damaged and never walk again as his legs were smashed to smithereens. The doctor then promised me that they were going to do everything that they possibly could to try and save Raymond and that surgeons were already preparing to take him down to theatre as he needed many operations which would take them right through the night and into the following morning before they were finished.

He then strongly advised me to go home with my family as there was nothing I could do and that it would be far better for me to be sitting in a warm home with others than in a draughty corridor on my own. I was also told not to phone until after six o'clock the following morning as they wouldn't be able to tell me anything until then.

I don't even remember leaving the hospital or how we got back to my mam's house. I have no recollection of it whatsoever. All I remember is plonking myself down in the armchair and Lee running over and climbing onto my knee and giving me the biggest hug ever and kissing me to death. It was just what I needed from someone: a great big hug. As well as Lee being a proper little boy he was also very loving and affectionate and loved to be hugged and kissed by us and by others too.

Everyone else was chatting amongst themselves while my mam saw to the necessary phone calls that needed to be made including to Raymond's mam in Edinburgh as I wasn't in the right frame of mind to talk to anyone. All I could think about was Raymond. My mam's friend who was a policeman had also popped in as he had heard about the accident. He was one of those guys who was always way over the top and as loud as they come; he just didn't know when to stop and went on and on and on trying to be the big guy and the biggest clown ever. He showed no respect whatsoever to me or for Raymond that night and should've done especially under the circumstances as someone in his position should have known better. I was so desperate to get away from him for some peace and quiet as he had my head done in with all the noise he was making, but the only thing that was on my mind was all the operations that Raymond was facing.

I asked my mam if I could leave Lee with them for the night as I needed to go home and spend some time on my own and I would be back down first thing in the morning. I was also wanting to cry but kept fighting back the tears as I couldn't do it with everyone else being around as I wanted to be in private, so no one would ever know how I was feeling in case anyone passed comment and saw me as being weak. But most of all, I desperately felt the need to pray to God and I couldn't do it here as I wanted it to be private between him and me. So again no one would ever know.

My dad walked me home and I couldn't get there quick enough as I was frightened that I was going to lose sight of God in my mind. As soon as my dad left I went straight into the sitting room and broke down on the settee. I was still in shock; it was just like a nightmare and a horrible one at that, again never thinking for one minute that something like this would have happened to us. All that kept going over in my mind was how much Raymond was going to need a miracle if he were to survive the night.

Once I began to cry I found it difficult to stop. I just loved him so much. He wasn't just my husband; he was also my best friend and soulmate and I couldn't imagine or bear to think of my life without him in it. Raymond was a fighter and he certainly had the biggest fight of his life on his hands that night.

He always told me as long as Lee and I were alive that he'd always be there to take care of us. I believed every word he said and that's what I was hanging onto. I didn't feel bitter with God this time nor did I blame him for what had happened like I normally would have. Instead, I went down on my knees and prayed like I had never prayed before, asking for his help and to save Raymond for me and my little boy. I felt so guilty and bad in doing it and especially asking for so much because, after all, I had done nothing for God except slag him off which made me feel so ashamed – so I asked him to forgive me.

I remember hearing about the miracles that Jesus had performed from when I took myself off to church when I was young and also when my Nana Gardener took me to the mission hall with her. I had always felt this gap and a longing inside of me to find God in my life and yet I never knew why as I always put this brick wall up between us because of the many painful and bad times I'd been through. I think when many of us are faced with a life-or-death situation that God is always the one we turn to, whether we believe in him or not, hoping that he will hear our prayers and help us.

I can honestly say that throughout my life I had never turned to God in such a way as I did on that night, hoping he would hear me and answer my prayers. It had been a long night and I was just so relieved that I hadn't received any calls from the hospital which meant Raymond was still alive. I phoned as instructed after six in the morning and they told me that all the operations had gone according to plan but that he was still very critically ill and that it was still touch and go at this stage and they would fill me in on everything else when I got there.

That same morning I immediately phoned Mickey Gibson as I had forgotten to tell my mam to do it the night before. He was a good friend of ours from when Raymond worked at Kavli's cheese factory and Raymond had also been best man at his wedding ten months ago. He was devastated when I told him the news and so was his wife Sandra. He was always someone whom we could depend upon if we ever needed a helping hand. I asked if he would come into the hospital with me as I was frightened and couldn't face it on my own as I didn't know what to expect. I also knew I could trust Michael and that he would be honest in describing everything about Raymond's condition to me, leaving nothing out, so that I could assess the situation for myself.

As we arrived at the hospital and made our way down to the intensive care unit I could feel my heart pumping fifty to the dozen and began to feel sick. I held tightly onto Michael's arm as we entered the room and the nurse pointed to where Raymond was.

At first I found it nerve-racking as all I could hear were the sounds of machines at work. No matter how bad I knew the situation was and also the amount of injuries he had received, until you are actually there at the bedside somehow you are still never prepared for what you about to hear and see. I was so desperate to hold Raymond's hand and to touch him, but I didn't dare until I knew all the facts from the nurses and from Michael's information. It was so hard just standing there feeling helpless, knowing that there was nothing I could do to help him.

Michael's immediate reaction said it all to me as he was very quiet and didn't speak and I could tell how shocked and upset he was at what he saw. The nurses told me roughly the same as what the doctors had told me on the phone that morning, so while we were waiting for the consultant to arrive Michael eventually explained that he would never have known it was Raymond if the nurses hadn't pointed him out to him as he was totally unrecognisable. This was simply because he was bandaged from head to foot. He reckoned both his face and head were treble the size despite the bandages being on and that his forehead stuck out like a frog. There were also thick pads on his eyes as they were bleeding internally and partially covering his upper cheeks. He was unconscious, on a life support machine and the only flesh you could see were his lower cheeks, jaw, upper arms and chest which were covered with different electrodes and tubes. Both legs were up in stirrups and were heavily bandaged from the thighs to his feet.

I was still trying to digest this and get my head around what Michael had just said when in walked the consultant. I was dreading what he was going to say after hearing all that from Michael. He took me step by step through every injury Raymond had received and all the operations performed from the blood clot on the brain, fractured skull, other broken bones in the head and the amount of multiple fractures to his thighs, knees and lower legs and how they rebuilt them with nuts, bolts, screws, pins and rods as well as having bone grafts. But the biggest blow of all was yet to come when he told me that one side of Raymond's brain was bruised which would unfortunately cause him to have brain damage, but how severe they didn't know.

I was then asked again how had the accident happened and when I said all I knew was that the police said he'd been hit by a car, not one of the consultants or doctors who were involved with Raymond's case believed it for one minute and said it had to at least have been a ten ton truck for the amount of damages and horrific injuries he'd received as it was one of the worst cases they had dealt with in a number of years. They were all more than convinced and said that there had to be more to it as they dealt with people getting knocked over practically every week and somehow this one didn't seem to fall into that category and they felt something else must have happened.

So here I was not just faced with a critically ill and brain-damaged husband who was fighting for his life and might not survive, but also a horrific car accident that seemed to have been much worse than what we had been told and was possibly being covered up, hoping that the truth wouldn't be exposed.

It's just as well we don't know what's around the corner or what the future has in store for us as once again here I was with my life turned upside down within a matter of hours. Just yesterday we thought we had the world at our fingertips and couldn't have been happier but instead I'm standing at his bedside in the intensive care unit telling him to fight with all his might and not to give up as we loved him so much and couldn't bear the thought of being here without him. "So you have to survive for us, Raymond," I said. "Do you hear me? You must survive!"

I stayed with him all day and later in the evening Michael came back to pick me up. I was totally broken hearted and felt bad leaving him there like that but there was nothing more I could do or say. I just felt so helpless. Michael took me back to my mam's as I was so desperate to see Lee and just wanted to hold him in my arms. I also felt I needed to have one more night on my own as there was so much going through my head and I couldn't have coped with Lee being there. Michael then took me up and left.

As soon as I shut the door I burst into tears. My head was all over the place and all I could think about was Raymond lying there without me by his side – but the hospital was very strict and you weren't allowed to stay overnight. So I quietly sat down on the settee with my head in my hands, wishing I had someone to talk to who could understand how I was feeling as I just wanted some reassurance. Then I began to think about God again.

"Can you hear me, God?" I said quietly. "Can you hear me?"

I wanted to believe so much that he could. I then felt so strongly the need to go and kneel down in the middle of the room and to open my hands and place my arms out at either side of my body and pray. It was all so strange and yet somehow it felt as if it was the most natural thing for me to do. I still couldn't stop crying and kept apologizing to him and poured my heart out, telling him exactly how I felt as I was so worried in case I lost Raymond and explained to God how much we both needed his help. I even made a promise to him hoping he would hear and believe me as I meant every word in saying:

"That if you save Raymond for me and my little boy, I promise that I will search for you and when I find you I will dedicate my whole life to you God and do anything you ask of me."

I didn't know what else to do, so I placed Raymond into God's hands and asked him to take care of him for me and hoped and prayed that he would still allow us to have a future together no matter what the outcome may be as I would take care of him for the rest of my days if I was lucky enough for him to be spared.

Although I wasn't a true believer in God I was always a great believer in fate and believed what will be, will be, no matter what we want and hope for as it's not up to us, only the big man himself upstairs.

So now I will just have to remain strong and be patient as only time alone will tell!

... *This is far from the end of the story of my life as there is still so much more to tell, but that will follow in my sequel much later down the line.*